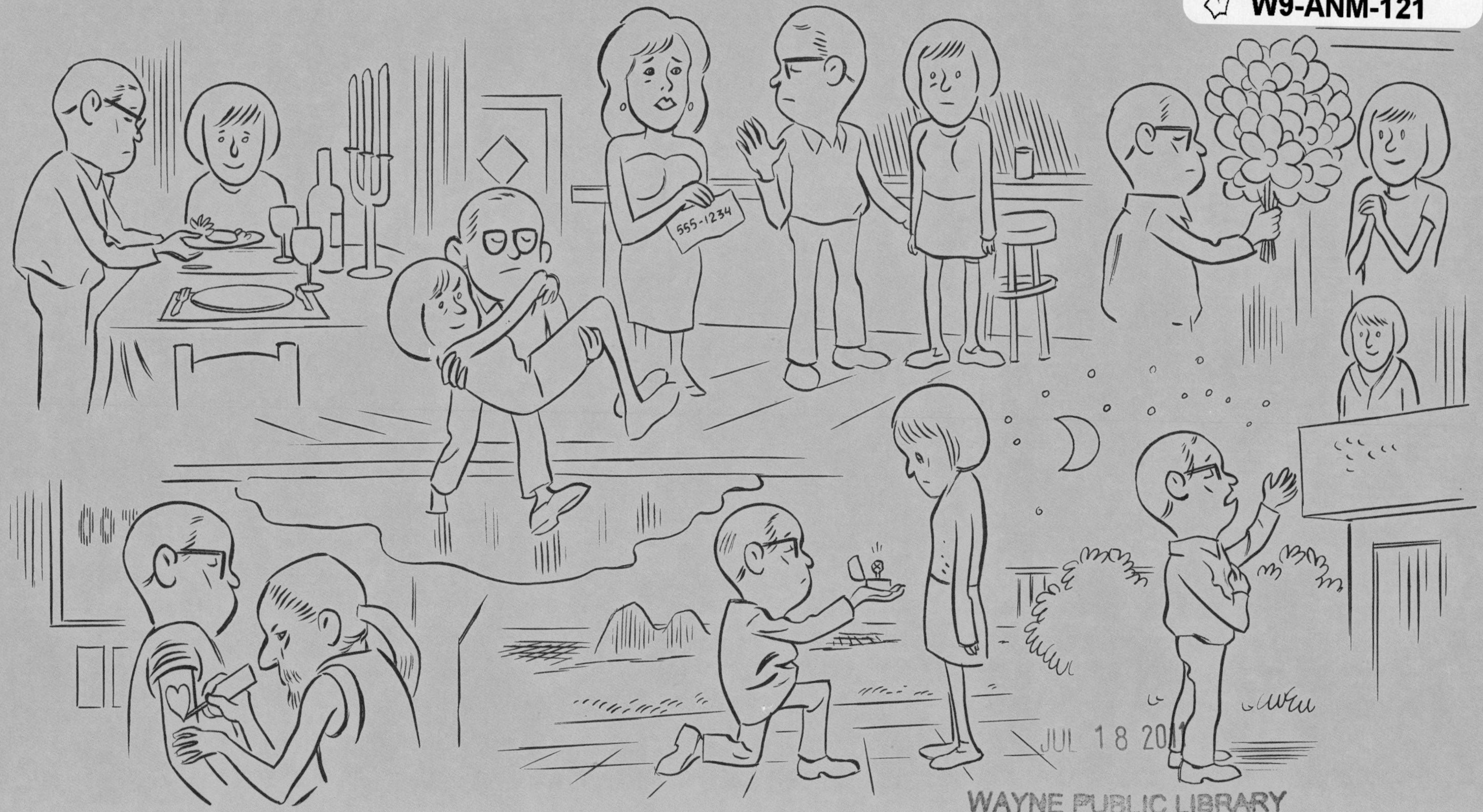
555-1234

mister wonderful

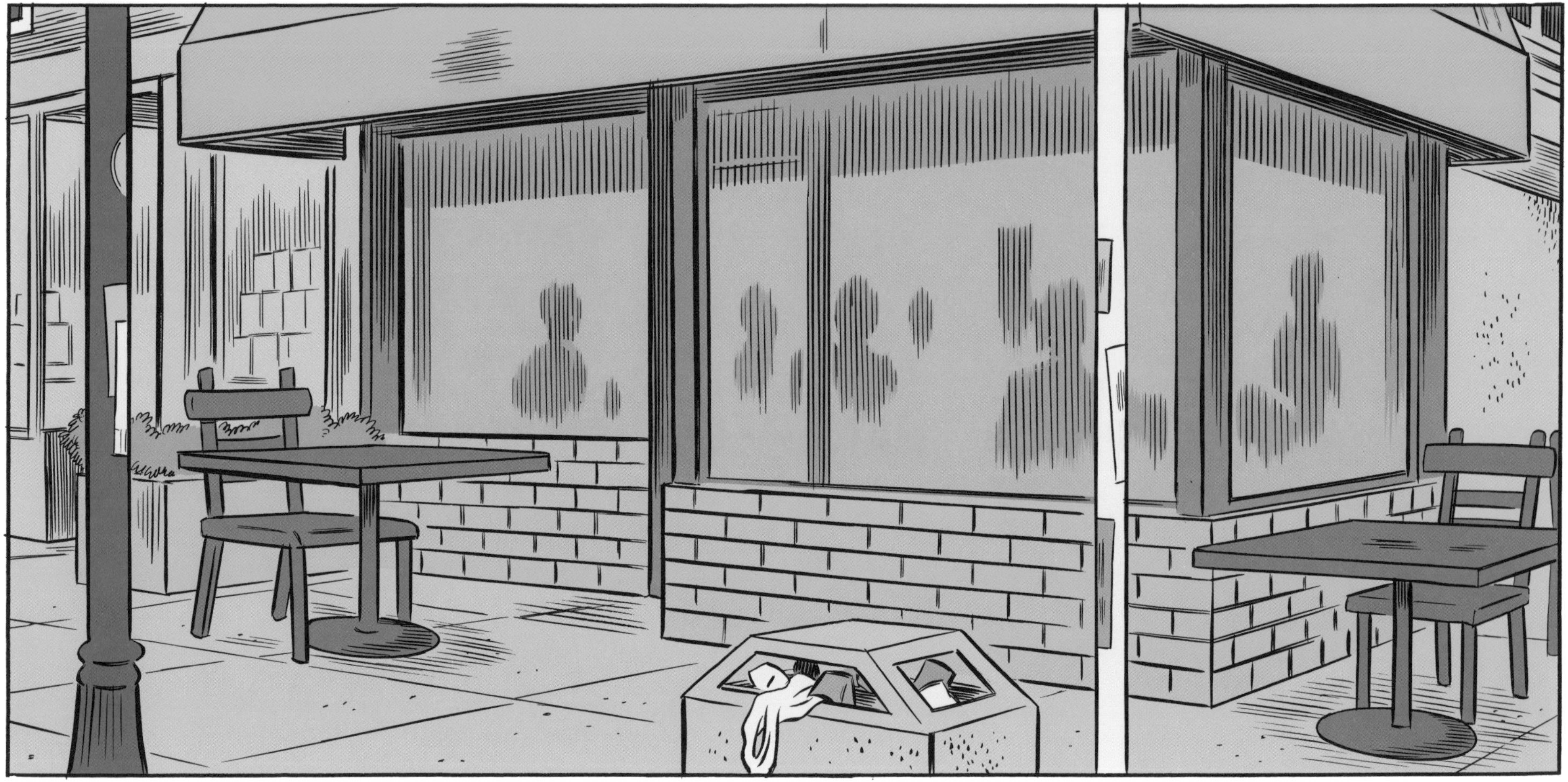

BY DANIEL CLOWES

PUBLISHED BY PANTHEON  NEW YORK

FOR ERIKA

 PUBLISHED IN THE UNITED STATES BY PANTHEON BOOKS, A DIVISION OF RANDOM HOUSE, INC., NEW YORK, AND IN CANADA BY RANDOM HOUSE OF CANADA LIMITED, TORONTO. PANTHEON BOOKS AND COLOPHON ARE REGISTERED TRADEMARKS OF RANDOM HOUSE, INC.

PORTIONS OF THIS WORK ORIGINALLY APPEARED IN *THE NEW YORK TIMES MAGAZINE*. IT HAS BEEN MODIFIED AND EXPANDED FOR THIS EDITION. THE SWEARING HAS BEEN LEFT IN #@$* FORM FOR AESTHETIC REASONS. SPECIAL THANKS TO SHEILA GLASER AND JAZZY JOHN KURAMOTO.

LIBRARY OF CONGRESS CATALOGING-IN-PUBLICATION DATA
CLOWES, DANIEL
MISTER WONDERFUL / DANIEL CLOWES.
P. CM.
ISBN 978-0-307-37813-2
1. GRAPHIC NOVELS. I. TITLE.
PN6727.C565M57 2011 741.5'973-DC22 2010035354

WWW.PANTHEONBOOKS.COM PRINTED IN SINGAPORE.
FIRST EDITION 9 8 7 6 5 4 3 2 1

6:09 PM

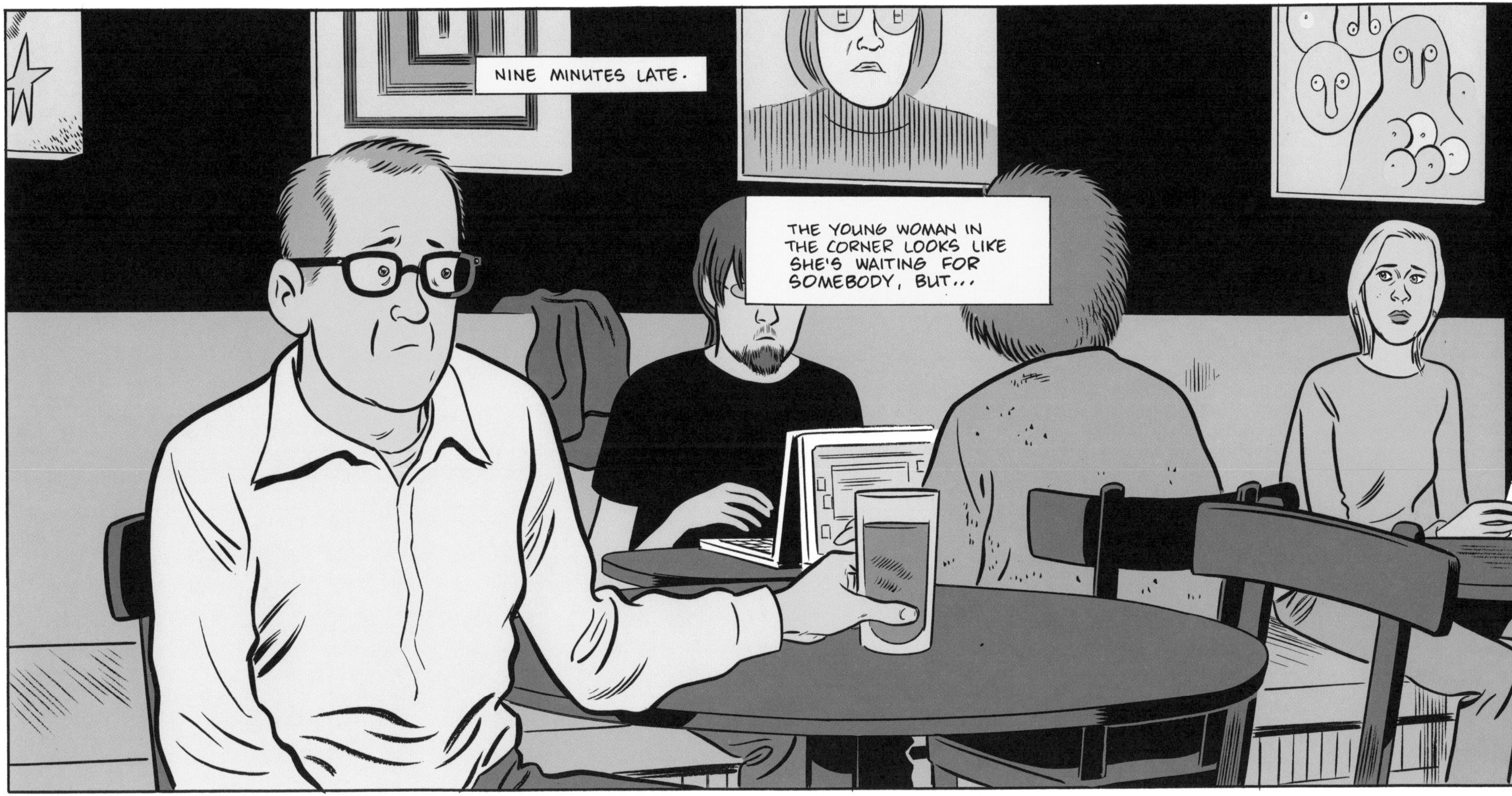
NINE MINUTES LATE.
THE YOUNG WOMAN IN THE CORNER LOOKS LIKE SHE'S WAITING FOR SOMEBODY, BUT...

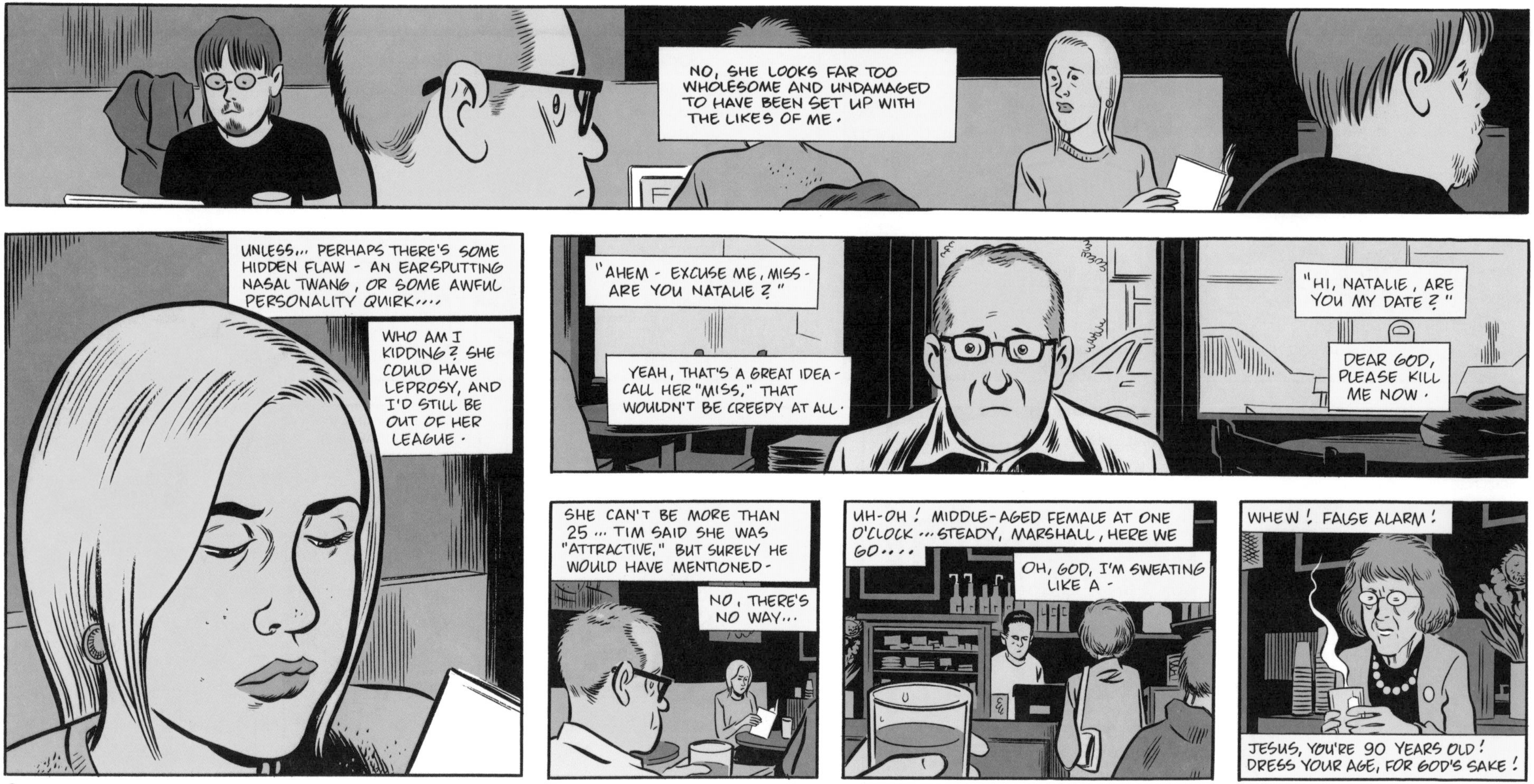
NO, SHE LOOKS FAR TOO WHOLESOME AND UNDAMAGED TO HAVE BEEN SET UP WITH THE LIKES OF ME.
UNLESS... PERHAPS THERE'S SOME HIDDEN FLAW - AN EARSPLITTING NASAL TWANG, OR SOME AWFUL PERSONALITY QUIRK....
WHO AM I KIDDING? SHE COULD HAVE LEPROSY, AND I'D STILL BE OUT OF HER LEAGUE.
"AHEM - EXCUSE ME, MISS - ARE YOU NATALIE?"
YEAH, THAT'S A GREAT IDEA - CALL HER "MISS," THAT WOULDN'T BE CREEPY AT ALL.
"HI, NATALIE, ARE YOU MY DATE?"
DEAR GOD, PLEASE KILL ME NOW.
SHE CAN'T BE MORE THAN 25 ... TIM SAID SHE WAS "ATTRACTIVE," BUT SURELY HE WOULD HAVE MENTIONED -
NO, THERE'S NO WAY...
UH-OH! MIDDLE-AGED FEMALE AT ONE O'CLOCK ... STEADY, MARSHALL, HERE WE GO....
OH, GOD, I'M SWEATING LIKE A -
WHEW! FALSE ALARM!
JESUS, YOU'RE 90 YEARS OLD! DRESS YOUR AGE, FOR GOD'S SAKE!

ULP! UNDAMAGED BLONDIE'S LOOKING THIS WAY. COULD IT REALLY BE?

WHAT'S SHE READING?

AN INCONVENIENT TRUTH — AL GORE — USED

PERFECT! I'M OPPOSED TO GLOBAL WARMING, TOO!

NO W... DU...

DUDE, ARE YOU SERIOUS?

NO... NO, BUT DUDE, IF YOU THINK I'M LYING...

LOOK, I'LL SWEAR ON LI... A STACK OF M... BIBLES, DUDE

JESUS! SHUT UP!

YEAH, NO, OF COURSE ...OF COURSE I TOL... HIM... I SAID I TO... HIM, BUT IF YOU'RE S... I TOOK CREDIT FOR...

WHAT'S HAPPENED TO OUR CIVILIZATION? WHEN DID IT BECOME OKAY FOR NON-CRAZY PEOPLE TO BABBLE THEIR PERSONAL NONSENSE IN PUBLIC?

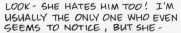

LOOK — SHE HATES HIM TOO! I'M USUALLY THE ONLY ONE WHO EVEN SEEMS TO NOTICE, BUT SHE—

THAT'... HARSH

WHERE WERE YOU? I'VE BEEN SITTING HERE FOR—

SORRY, BABE — TWO MORE SECONDS, OKAY?

EIGHTEEN MINUTES LATE. I'M STARTING TO—

OH DEAR GOD.

9.

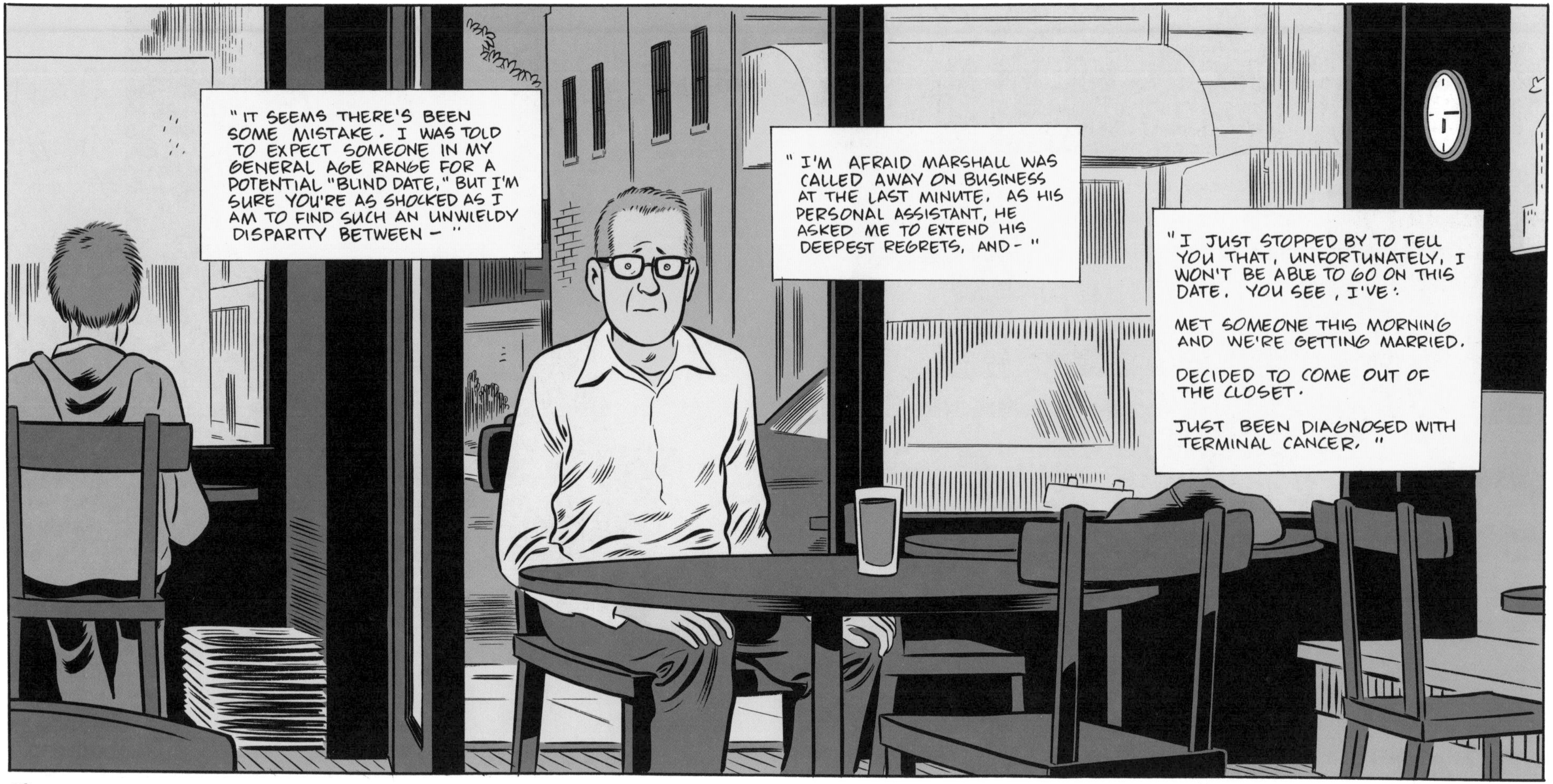
"IT SEEMS THERE'S BEEN SOME MISTAKE. I WAS TOLD TO EXPECT SOMEONE IN MY GENERAL AGE RANGE FOR A POTENTIAL "BLIND DATE," BUT I'M SURE YOU'RE AS SHOCKED AS I AM TO FIND SUCH AN UNWIELDY DISPARITY BETWEEN –"
"I'M AFRAID MARSHALL WAS CALLED AWAY ON BUSINESS AT THE LAST MINUTE. AS HIS PERSONAL ASSISTANT, HE ASKED ME TO EXTEND HIS DEEPEST REGRETS, AND –"
"I JUST STOPPED BY TO TELL YOU THAT, UNFORTUNATELY, I WON'T BE ABLE TO GO ON THIS DATE. YOU SEE, I'VE:
MET SOMEONE THIS MORNING AND WE'RE GETTING MARRIED.
DECIDED TO COME OUT OF THE CLOSET.
JUST BEEN DIAGNOSED WITH TERMINAL CANCER."

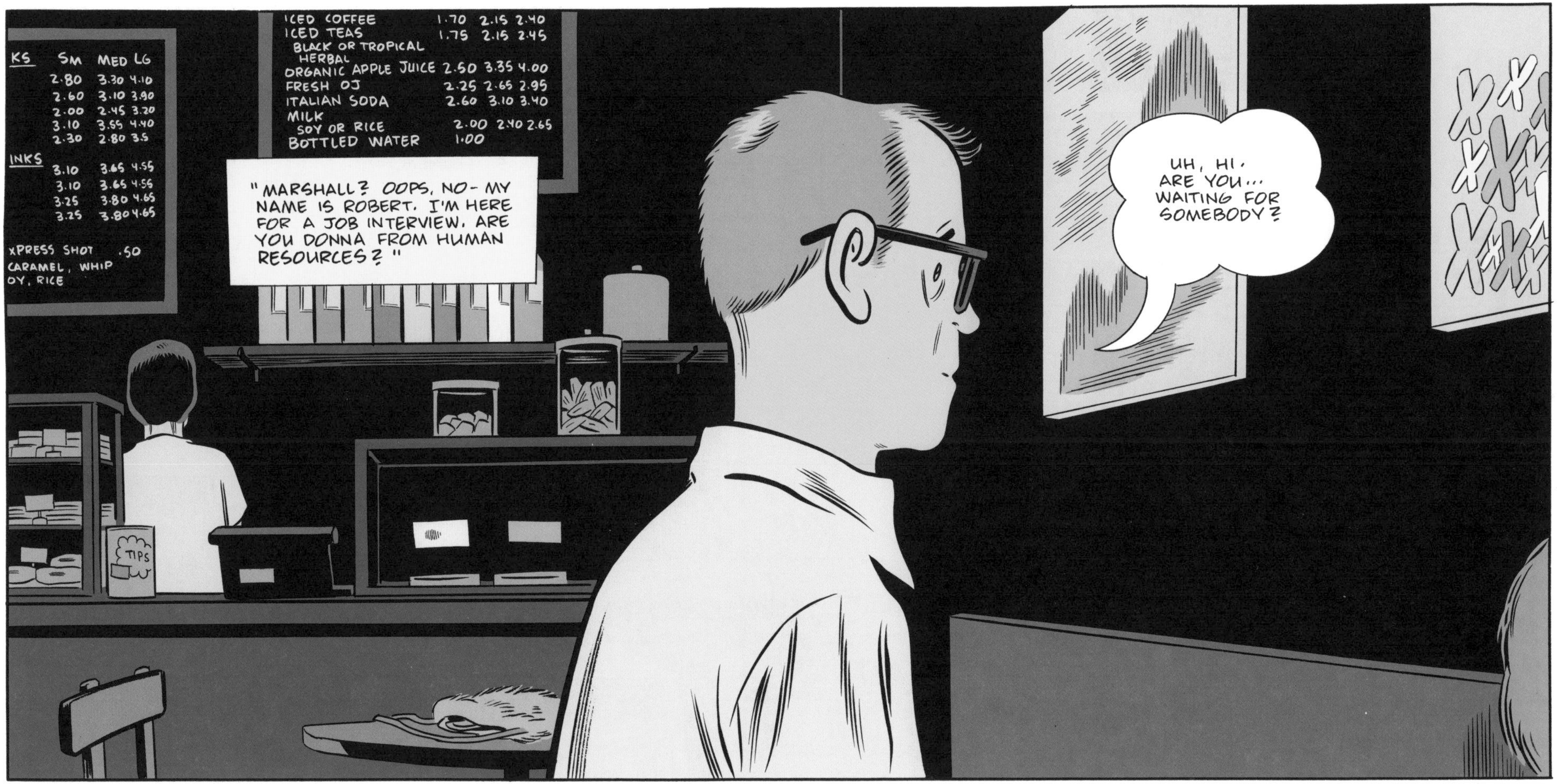
"MARSHALL? OOPS, NO- MY NAME IS ROBERT. I'M HERE FOR A JOB INTERVIEW. ARE YOU DONNA FROM HUMAN RESOURCES?"
UH, HI. ARE YOU... WAITING FOR SOMEBODY?
KS SM MED LG
2.80 3.30 4.10
2.60 3.10 3.90
2.00 2.45 3.20
3.10 3.55 4.40
2.30 2.80 3.5
INKS 3.10 3.65 4.55
3.10 3.65 4.55
3.25 3.80 4.65
3.25 3.80 4.65
XPRESS SHOT .50
CARAMEL, WHIP
OY, RICE
ICED COFFEE 1.70 2.15 2.40
ICED TEAS 1.75 2.15 2.45
BLACK OR TROPICAL
HERBAL
ORGANIC APPLE JUICE 2.50 3.35 4.00
FRESH OJ 2.25 2.65 2.95
ITALIAN SODA 2.60 3.10 3.40
MILK
SOY OR RICE 2.00 2.40 2.65
BOTTLED WATER 1.00
TIPS

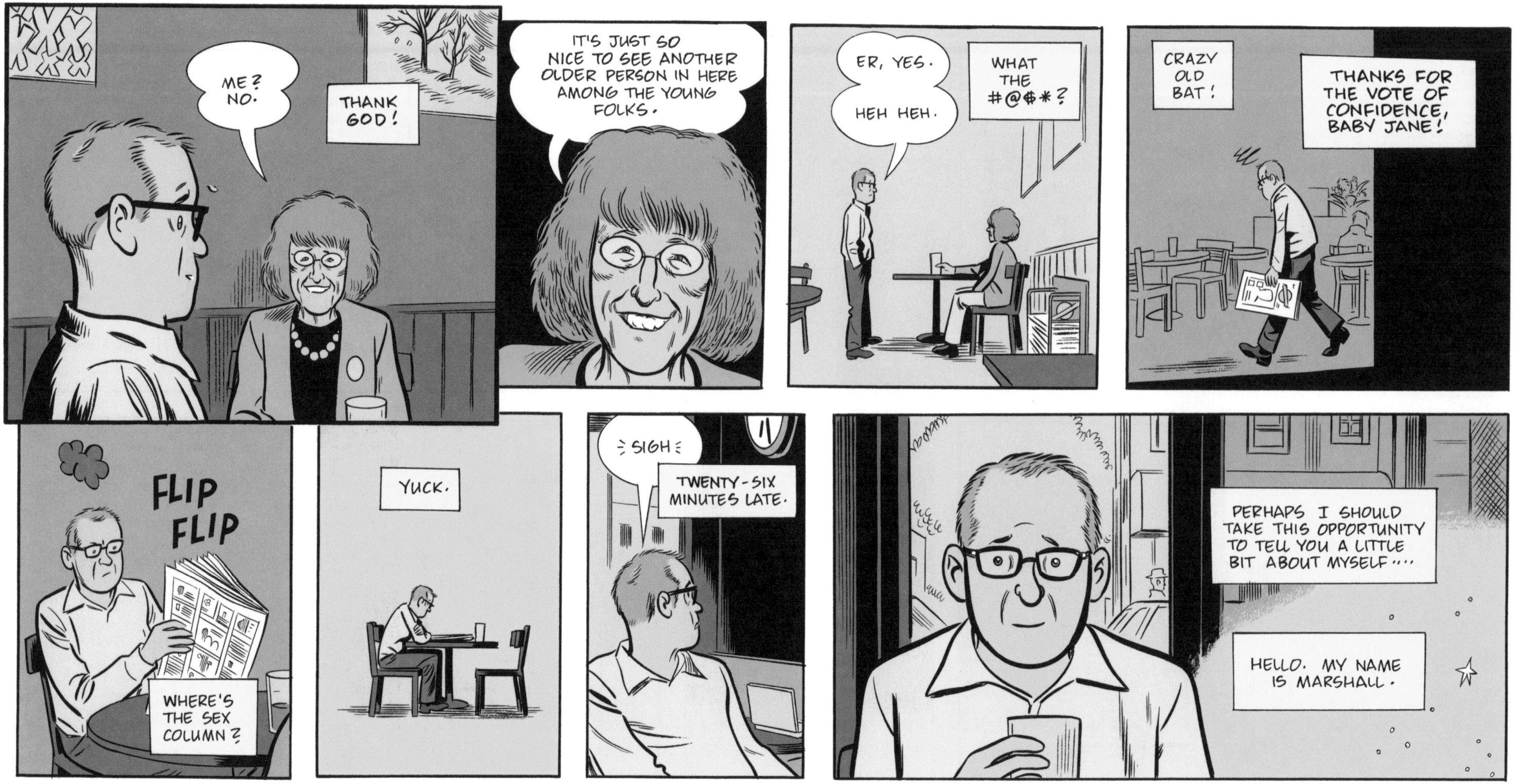
ME? NO.
THANK GOD!
IT'S JUST SO NICE TO SEE ANOTHER OLDER PERSON IN HERE AMONG THE YOUNG FOLKS.
ER, YES.
HEH HEH.
WHAT THE #@$*?
CRAZY OLD BAT!
THANKS FOR THE VOTE OF CONFIDENCE, BABY JANE!
FLIP FLIP
WHERE'S THE SEX COLUMN?
YUCK.
SIGH
TWENTY-SIX MINUTES LATE.
PERHAPS I SHOULD TAKE THIS OPPORTUNITY TO TELL YOU A LITTLE BIT ABOUT MYSELF....
HELLO. MY NAME IS MARSHALL.

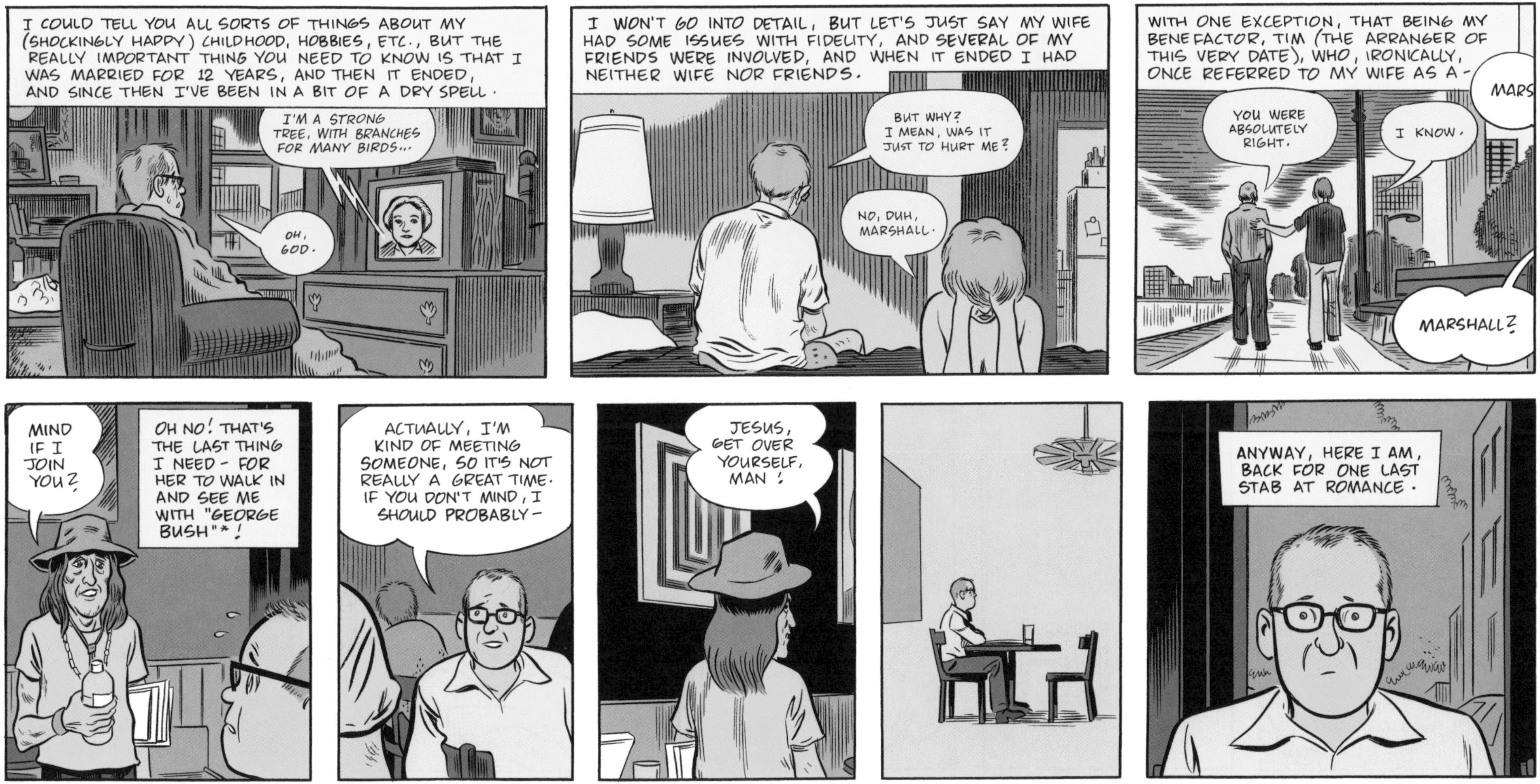
I COULD TELL YOU ALL SORTS OF THINGS ABOUT MY (SHOCKINGLY HAPPY) CHILDHOOD, HOBBIES, ETC., BUT THE REALLY IMPORTANT THING YOU NEED TO KNOW IS THAT I WAS MARRIED FOR 12 YEARS, AND THEN IT ENDED, AND SINCE THEN I'VE BEEN IN A BIT OF A DRY SPELL.
I'M A STRONG TREE, WITH BRANCHES FOR MANY BIRDS...
OH, GOD.
I WON'T GO INTO DETAIL, BUT LET'S JUST SAY MY WIFE HAD SOME ISSUES WITH FIDELITY, AND SEVERAL OF MY FRIENDS WERE INVOLVED, AND WHEN IT ENDED I HAD NEITHER WIFE NOR FRIENDS.
BUT WHY? I MEAN, WAS IT JUST TO HURT ME?
NO, DUH, MARSHALL.
WITH ONE EXCEPTION, THAT BEING MY BENEFACTOR, TIM (THE ARRANGER OF THIS VERY DATE), WHO, IRONICALLY, ONCE REFERRED TO MY WIFE AS A-
YOU WERE ABSOLUTELY RIGHT.
I KNOW.
MARS
MARSHALL?
MIND IF I JOIN YOU?
OH NO! THAT'S THE LAST THING I NEED - FOR HER TO WALK IN AND SEE ME WITH "GEORGE BUSH"*!
ACTUALLY, I'M KIND OF MEETING SOMEONE, SO IT'S NOT REALLY A GREAT TIME. IF YOU DON'T MIND, I SHOULD PROBABLY-
JESUS, GET OVER YOURSELF, MAN!
ANYWAY, HERE I AM, BACK FOR ONE LAST STAB AT ROMANCE.

*SO NICKNAMED IN 2006 FOR HIS RELENTLESS INVOCATION OF THIS CATCHALL NEMESIS.

MISTER W

ONDERFUL

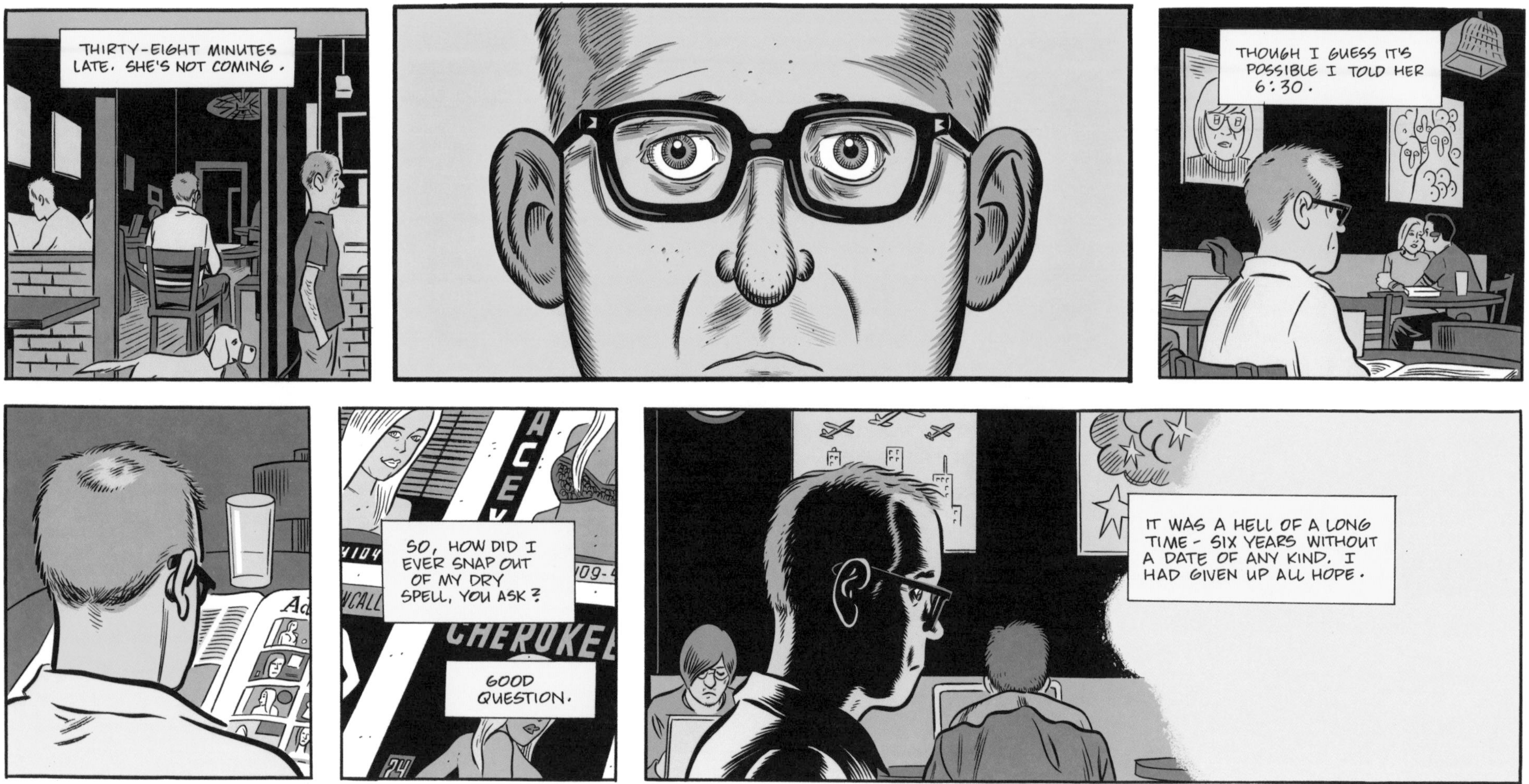
THIRTY-EIGHT MINUTES LATE. SHE'S NOT COMING.
THOUGH I GUESS IT'S POSSIBLE I TOLD HER 6:30.
SO, HOW DID I EVER SNAP OUT OF MY DRY SPELL, YOU ASK?
GOOD QUESTION.
CHEROKEE
IT WAS A HELL OF A LONG TIME - SIX YEARS WITHOUT A DATE OF ANY KIND. I HAD GIVEN UP ALL HOPE.

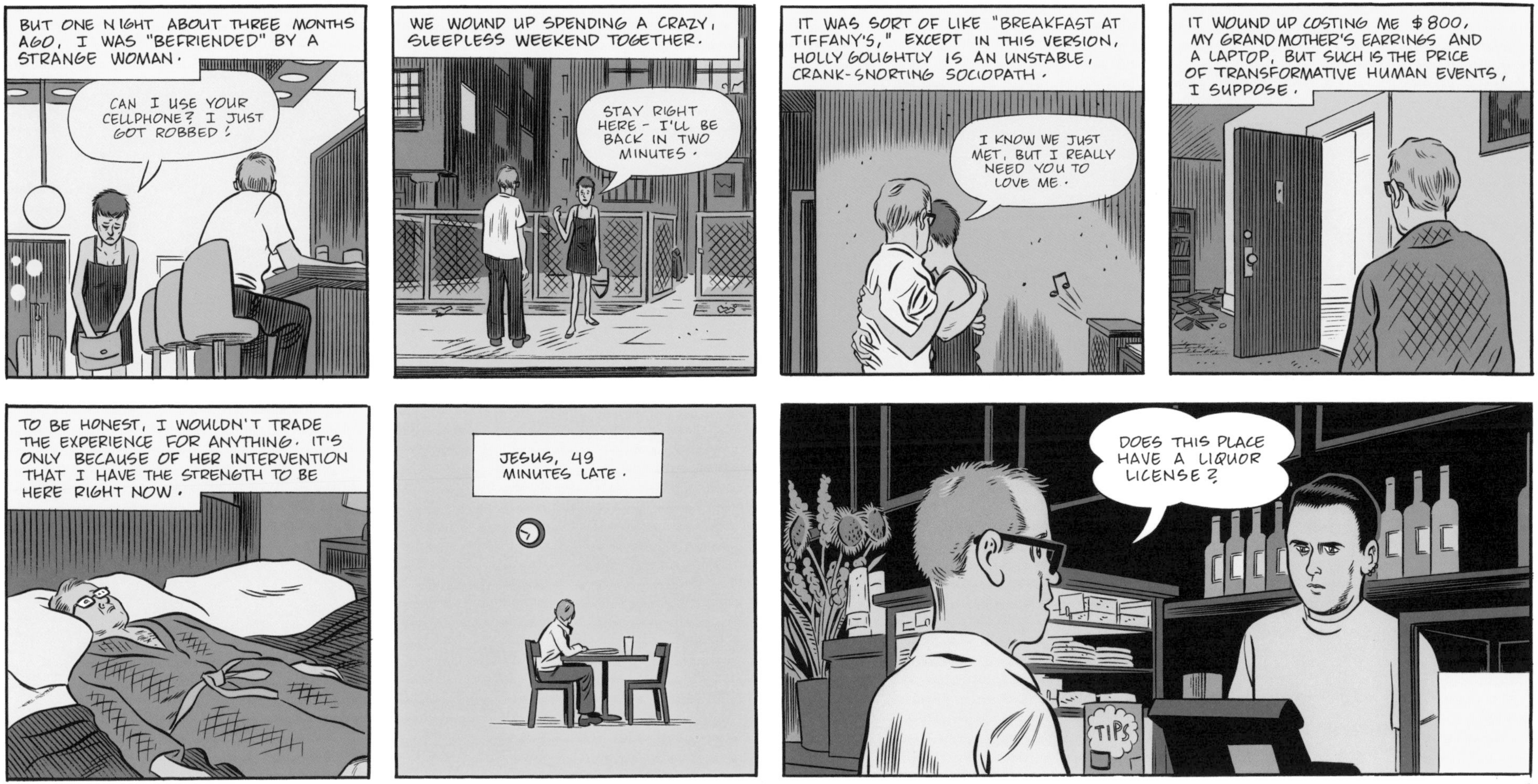
BUT ONE NIGHT ABOUT THREE MONTHS AGO, I WAS "BEFRIENDED" BY A STRANGE WOMAN.
CAN I USE YOUR CELLPHONE? I JUST GOT ROBBED!
WE WOUND UP SPENDING A CRAZY, SLEEPLESS WEEKEND TOGETHER.
STAY RIGHT HERE - I'LL BE BACK IN TWO MINUTES.
IT WAS SORT OF LIKE "BREAKFAST AT TIFFANY'S," EXCEPT IN THIS VERSION, HOLLY GOLIGHTLY IS AN UNSTABLE, CRANK-SNORTING SOCIOPATH.
I KNOW WE JUST MET, BUT I REALLY NEED YOU TO LOVE ME.
IT WOUND UP COSTING ME $800, MY GRANDMOTHER'S EARRINGS AND A LAPTOP, BUT SUCH IS THE PRICE OF TRANSFORMATIVE HUMAN EVENTS, I SUPPOSE.
TO BE HONEST, I WOULDN'T TRADE THE EXPERIENCE FOR ANYTHING. IT'S ONLY BECAUSE OF HER INTERVENTION THAT I HAVE THE STRENGTH TO BE HERE RIGHT NOW.
JESUS, 49 MINUTES LATE.
DOES THIS PLACE HAVE A LIQUOR LICENSE?
TIPS

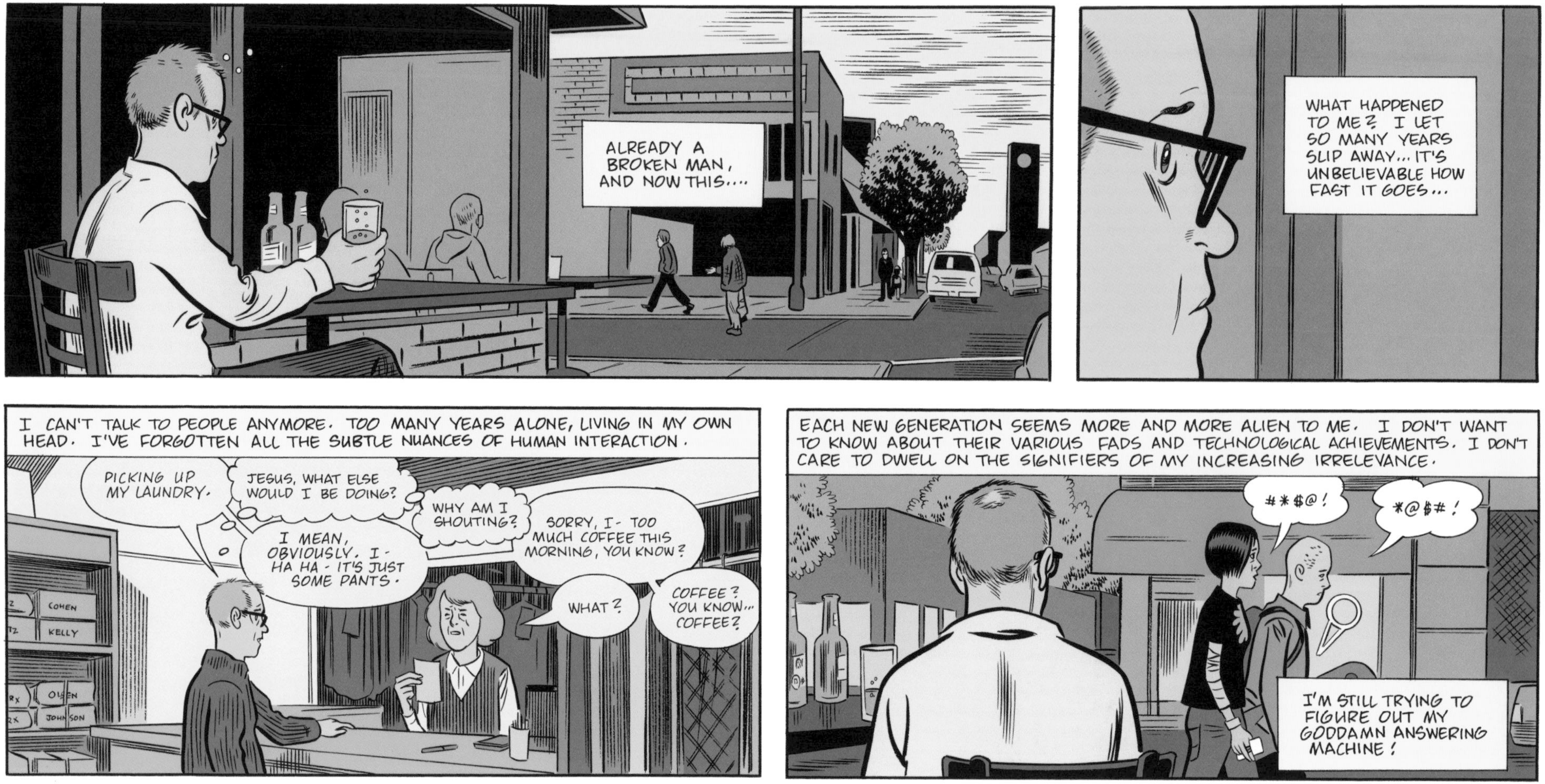

ALREADY A BROKEN MAN, AND NOW THIS....
WHAT HAPPENED TO ME? I LET SO MANY YEARS SLIP AWAY... IT'S UNBELIEVABLE HOW FAST IT GOES...
I CAN'T TALK TO PEOPLE ANYMORE. TOO MANY YEARS ALONE, LIVING IN MY OWN HEAD. I'VE FORGOTTEN ALL THE SUBTLE NUANCES OF HUMAN INTERACTION.
PICKING UP MY LAUNDRY.
JESUS, WHAT ELSE WOULD I BE DOING?
I MEAN, OBVIOUSLY. I- HA HA - IT'S JUST SOME PANTS.
WHY AM I SHOUTING?
SORRY, I- TOO MUCH COFFEE THIS MORNING, YOU KNOW?
WHAT?
COFFEE? YOU KNOW... COFFEE?
COHEN
KELLY
OLSEN
JOHNSON
EACH NEW GENERATION SEEMS MORE AND MORE ALIEN TO ME. I DON'T WANT TO KNOW ABOUT THEIR VARIOUS FADS AND TECHNOLOGICAL ACHIEVEMENTS. I DON'T CARE TO DWELL ON THE SIGNIFIERS OF MY INCREASING IRRELEVANCE.
#*$@!
*@$#!
I'M STILL TRYING TO FIGURE OUT MY GODDAMN ANSWERING MACHINE!

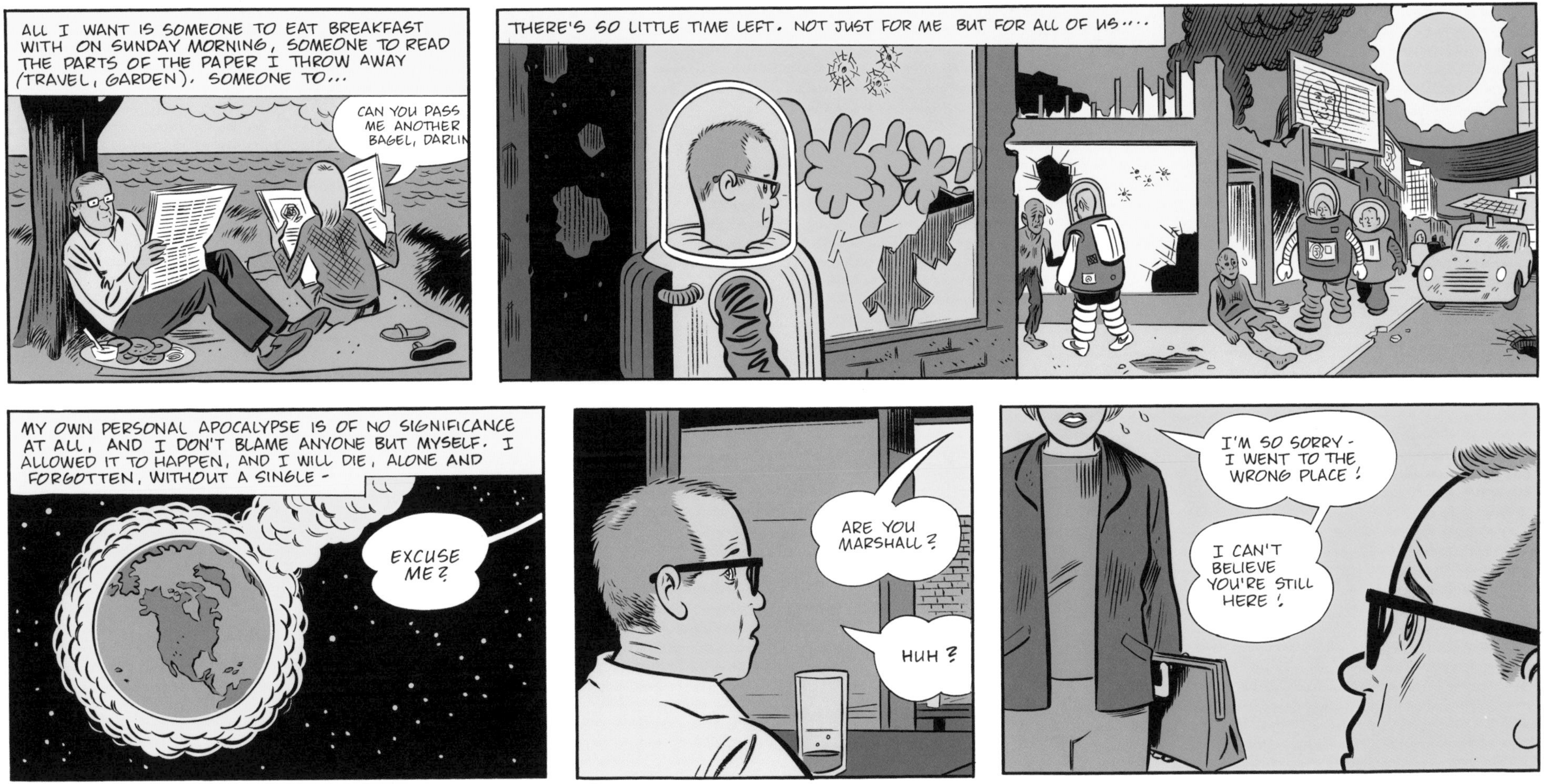
ALL I WANT IS SOMEONE TO EAT BREAKFAST WITH ON SUNDAY MORNING, SOMEONE TO READ THE PARTS OF THE PAPER I THROW AWAY (TRAVEL, GARDEN), SOMEONE TO...
CAN YOU PASS ME ANOTHER BAGEL, DARLIN
THERE'S SO LITTLE TIME LEFT. NOT JUST FOR ME BUT FOR ALL OF US....
MY OWN PERSONAL APOCALYPSE IS OF NO SIGNIFICANCE AT ALL, AND I DON'T BLAME ANYONE BUT MYSELF. I ALLOWED IT TO HAPPEN, AND I WILL DIE, ALONE AND FORGOTTEN, WITHOUT A SINGLE -
EXCUSE ME?
ARE YOU MARSHALL?
HUH?
I'M SO SORRY - I WENT TO THE WRONG PLACE!
I CAN'T BELIEVE YOU'RE STILL HERE!

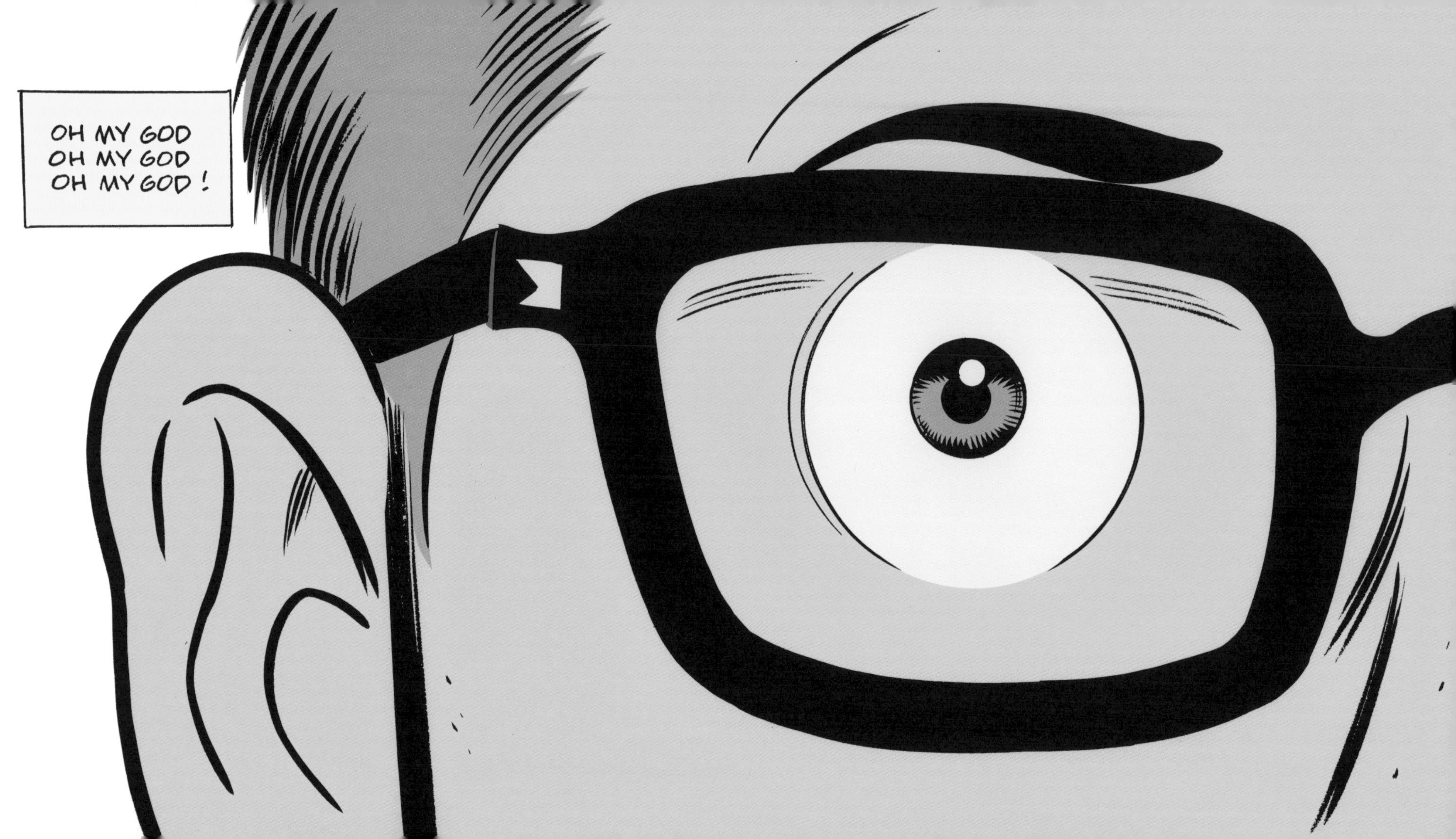
OH MY GOD
OH MY GOD
OH MY GOD !

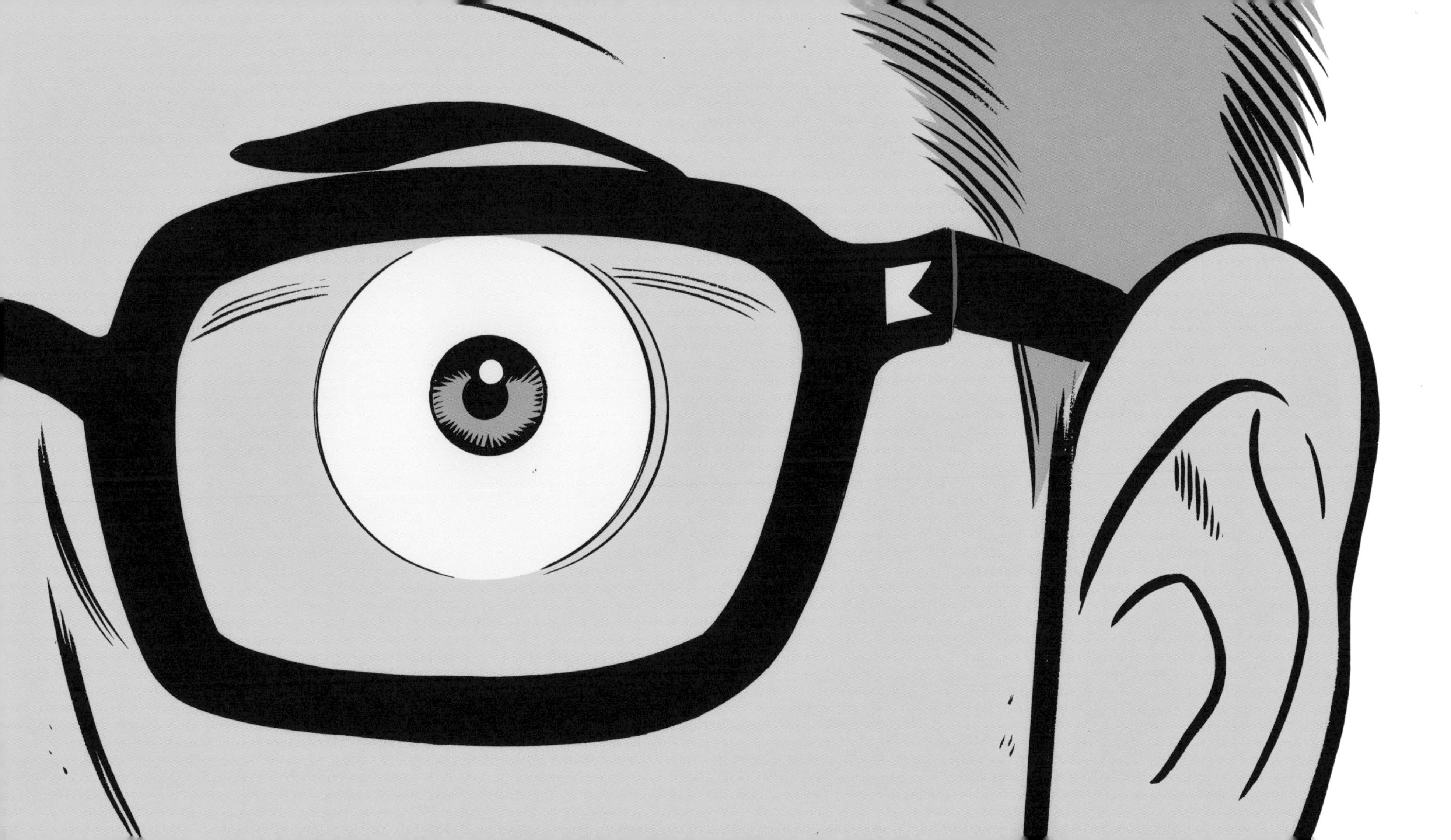

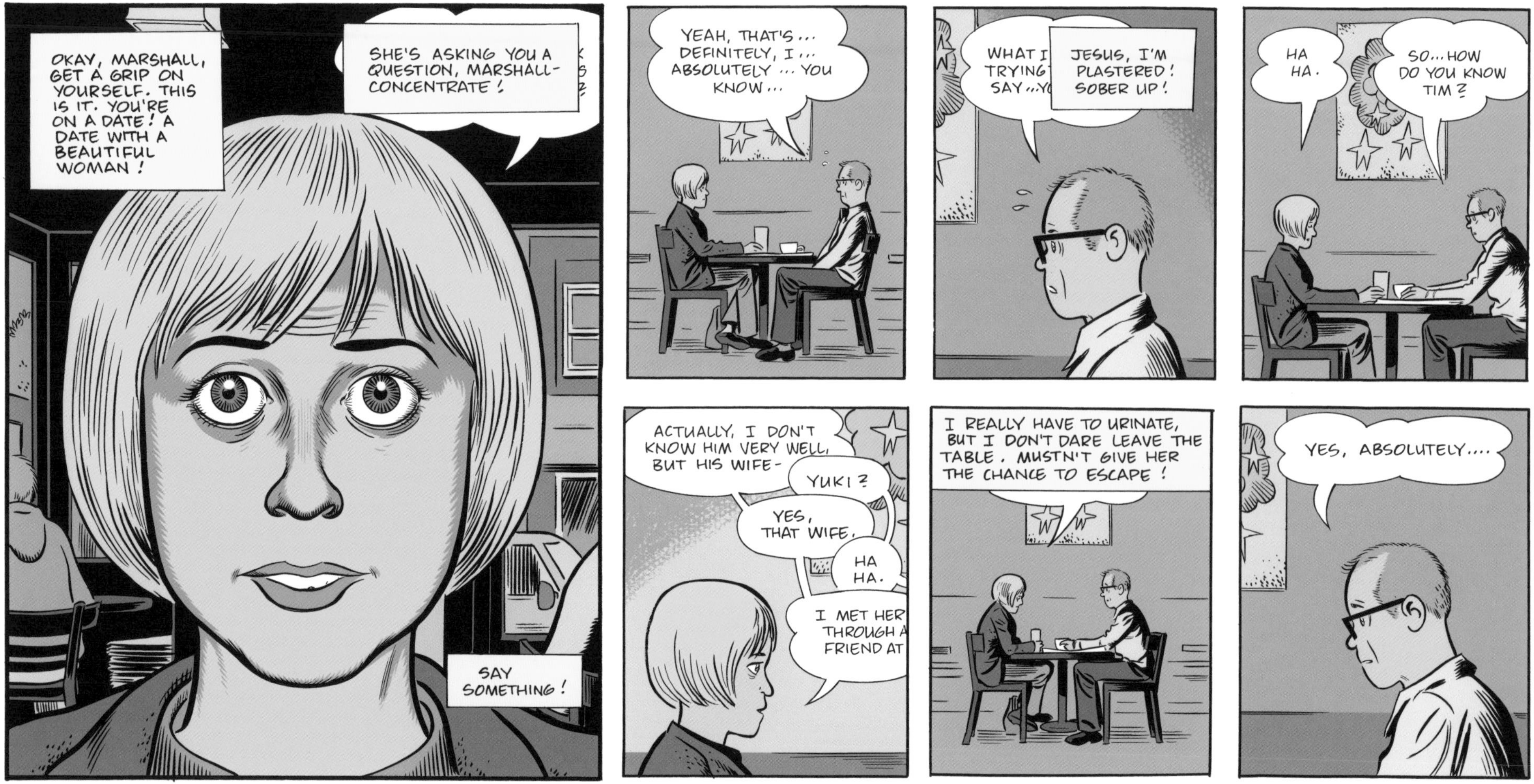
OKAY, MARSHALL, GET A GRIP ON YOURSELF. THIS IS IT. YOU'RE ON A DATE! A DATE WITH A BEAUTIFUL WOMAN!
SHE'S ASKING YOU A QUESTION, MARSHALL- CONCENTRATE!
SAY SOMETHING!
YEAH, THAT'S... DEFINITELY, I... ABSOLUTELY ... YOU KNOW...
WHAT I TRYING SAY...YO
JESUS, I'M PLASTERED! SOBER UP!
HA HA.
SO...HOW DO YOU KNOW TIM?
ACTUALLY, I DON'T KNOW HIM VERY WELL, BUT HIS WIFE-
YUKI?
YES, THAT WIFE.
HA HA.
I MET HER THROUGH A FRIEND AT
I REALLY HAVE TO URINATE, BUT I DON'T DARE LEAVE THE TABLE. MUSTN'T GIVE HER THE CHANCE TO ESCAPE!
YES, ABSOLUTELY....

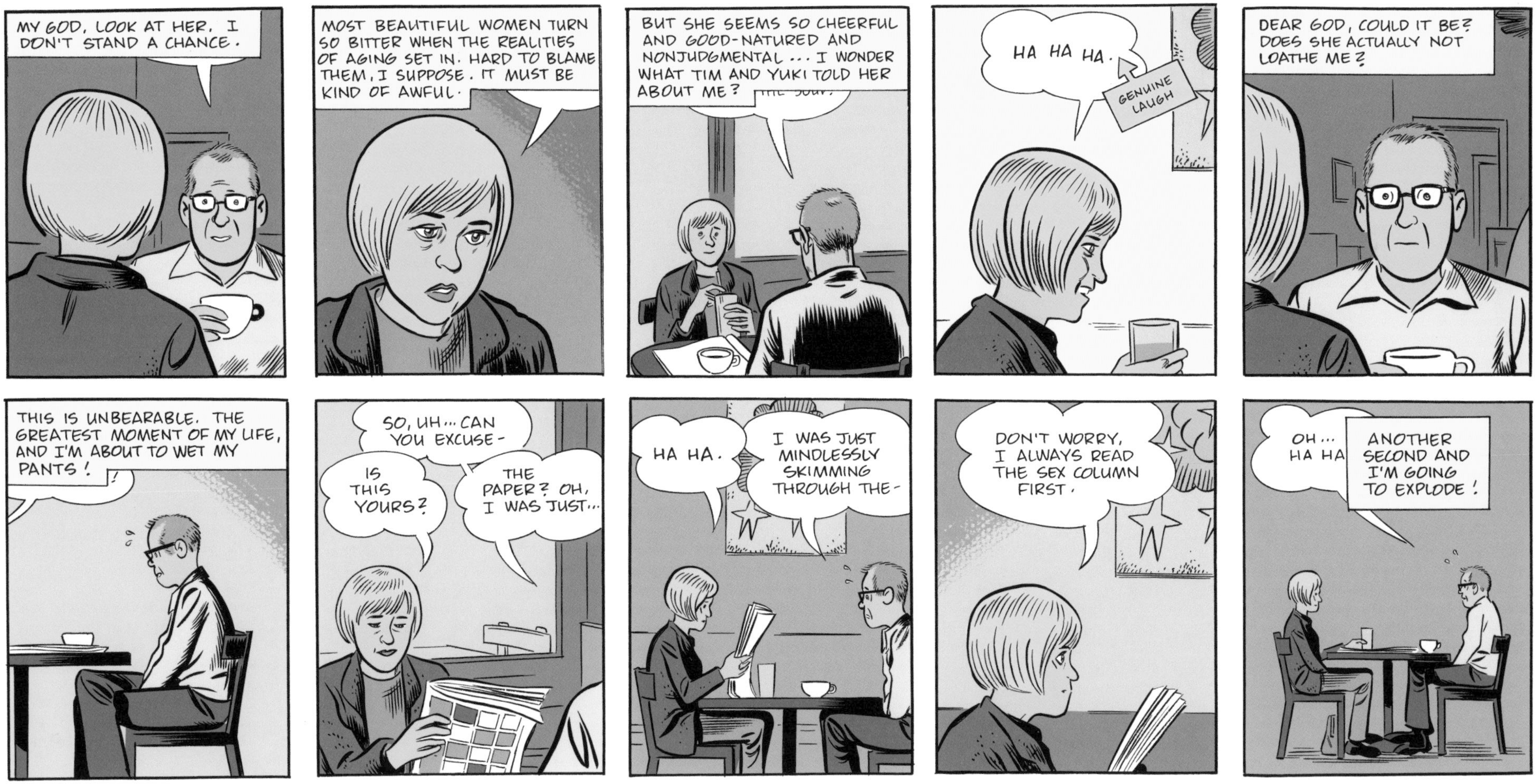

MY GOD, LOOK AT HER. I DON'T STAND A CHANCE.
MOST BEAUTIFUL WOMEN TURN SO BITTER WHEN THE REALITIES OF AGING SET IN. HARD TO BLAME THEM, I SUPPOSE. IT MUST BE KIND OF AWFUL.
BUT SHE SEEMS SO CHEERFUL AND GOOD-NATURED AND NONJUDGMENTAL ... I WONDER WHAT TIM AND YUKI TOLD HER ABOUT ME?
HA HA HA.
GENUINE LAUGH
DEAR GOD, COULD IT BE? DOES SHE ACTUALLY NOT LOATHE ME?
THIS IS UNBEARABLE. THE GREATEST MOMENT OF MY LIFE, AND I'M ABOUT TO WET MY PANTS!
SO, UH... CAN YOU EXCUSE-
IS THIS YOURS?
THE PAPER? OH, I WAS JUST...
HA HA.
I WAS JUST MINDLESSLY SKIMMING THROUGH THE-
DON'T WORRY, I ALWAYS READ THE SEX COLUMN FIRST.
OH... HA HA
ANOTHER SECOND AND I'M GOING TO EXPLODE!

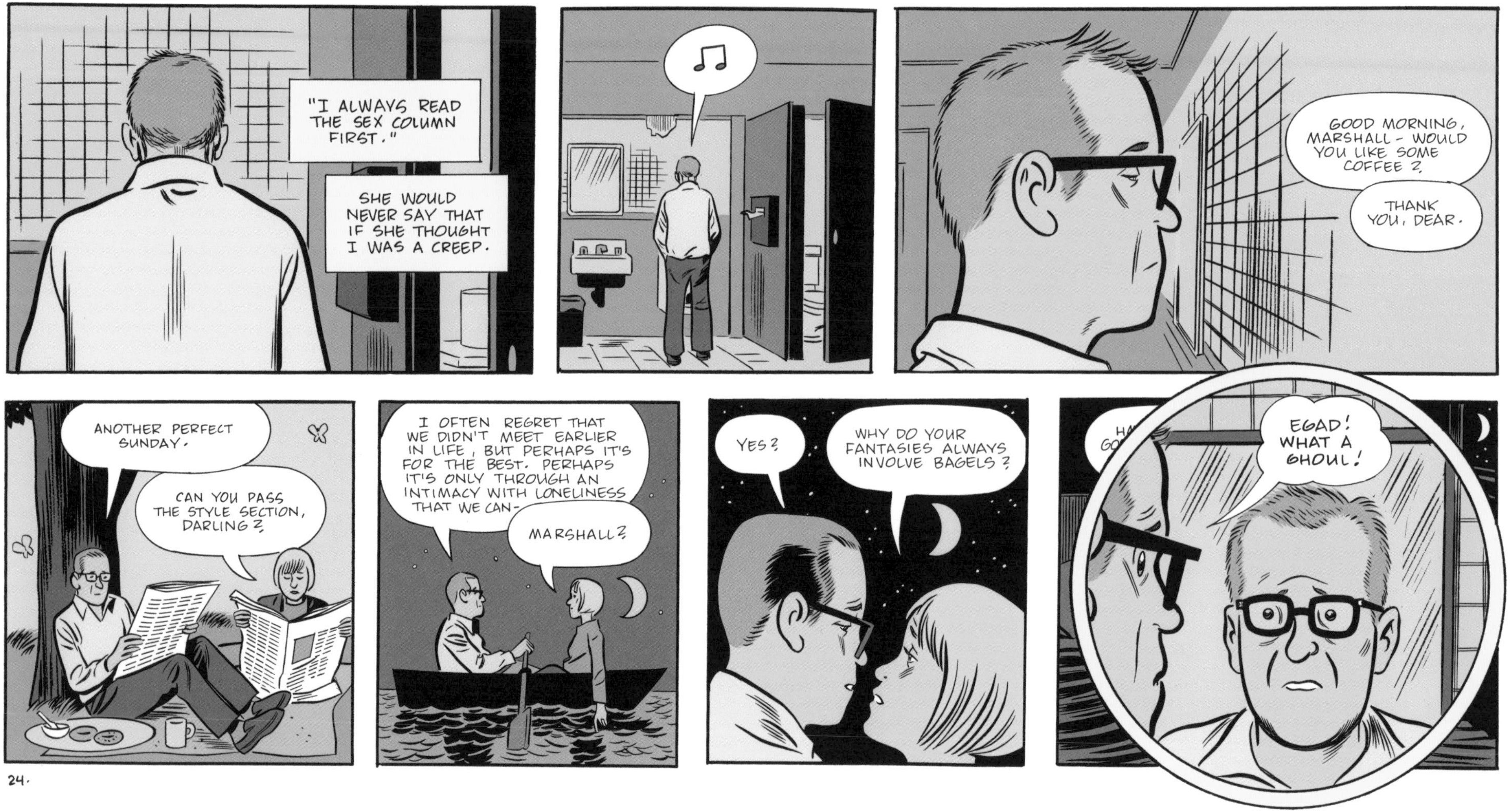
"I ALWAYS READ THE SEX COLUMN FIRST."
SHE WOULD NEVER SAY THAT IF SHE THOUGHT I WAS A CREEP.
♫
GOOD MORNING, MARSHALL - WOULD YOU LIKE SOME COFFEE?
THANK YOU, DEAR.
ANOTHER PERFECT SUNDAY.
CAN YOU PASS THE STYLE SECTION, DARLING?
I OFTEN REGRET THAT WE DIDN'T MEET EARLIER IN LIFE, BUT PERHAPS IT'S FOR THE BEST. PERHAPS IT'S ONLY THROUGH AN INTIMACY WITH LONELINESS THAT WE CAN-
MARSHALL?
YES?
WHY DO YOUR FANTASIES ALWAYS INVOLVE BAGELS?
EGAD! WHAT A GHOUL!

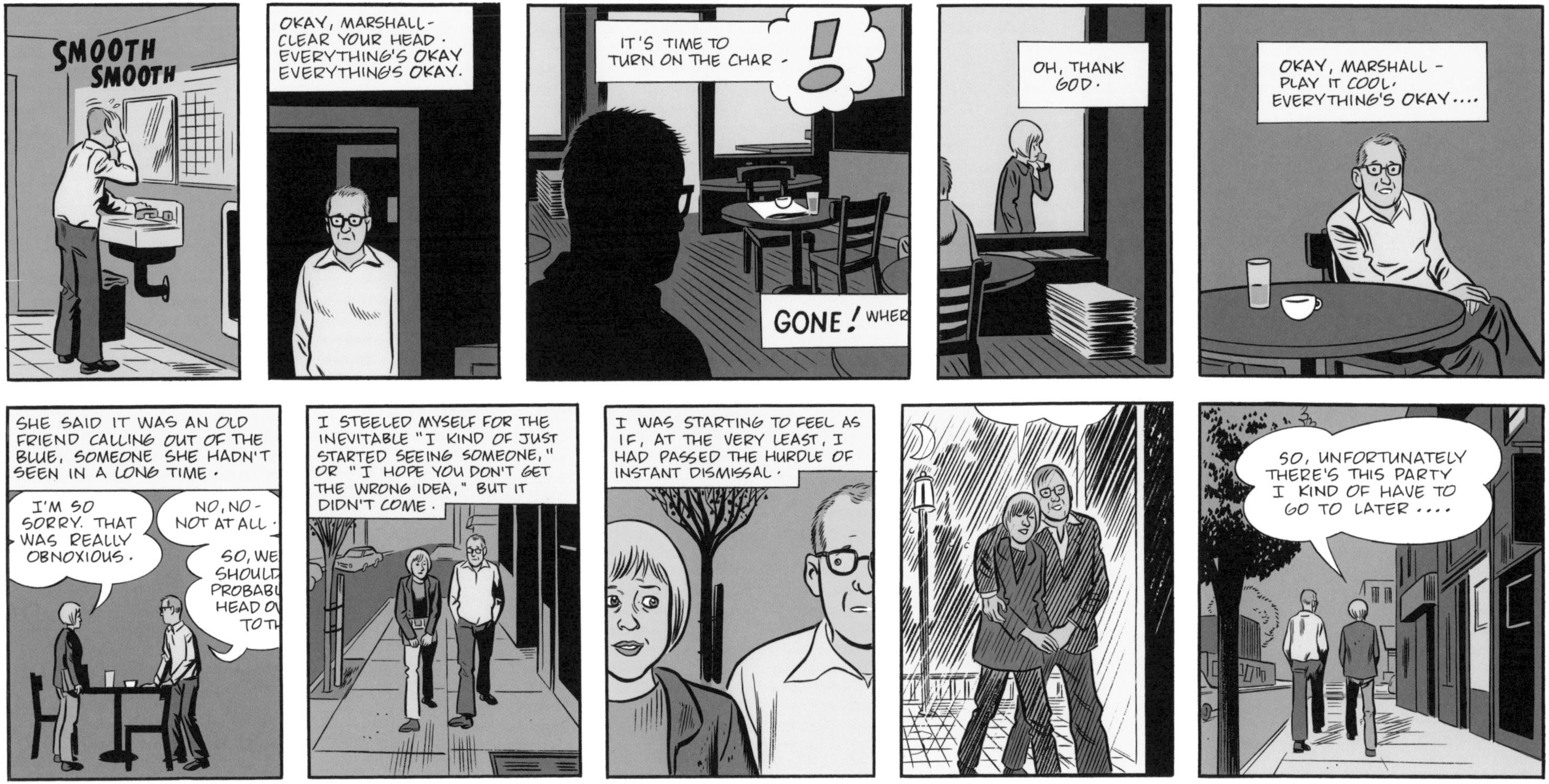

SMOOTH
SMOOTH
OKAY, MARSHALL- CLEAR YOUR HEAD. EVERYTHING'S OKAY EVERYTHING'S OKAY.
IT'S TIME TO TURN ON THE CHAR-
!
GONE! WHER
OH, THANK GOD.
OKAY, MARSHALL - PLAY IT COOL. EVERYTHING'S OKAY....
SHE SAID IT WAS AN OLD FRIEND CALLING OUT OF THE BLUE, SOMEONE SHE HADN'T SEEN IN A LONG TIME.
I'M SO SORRY. THAT WAS REALLY OBNOXIOUS.
NO, NO- NOT AT ALL.
SO, WE SHOULD PROBABL HEAD OV TO TH
I STEELED MYSELF FOR THE INEVITABLE "I KIND OF JUST STARTED SEEING SOMEONE," OR "I HOPE YOU DON'T GET THE WRONG IDEA," BUT IT DIDN'T COME.
I WAS STARTING TO FEEL AS IF, AT THE VERY LEAST, I HAD PASSED THE HURDLE OF INSTANT DISMISSAL.
SO, UNFORTUNATELY THERE'S THIS PARTY I KIND OF HAVE TO GO TO LATER....

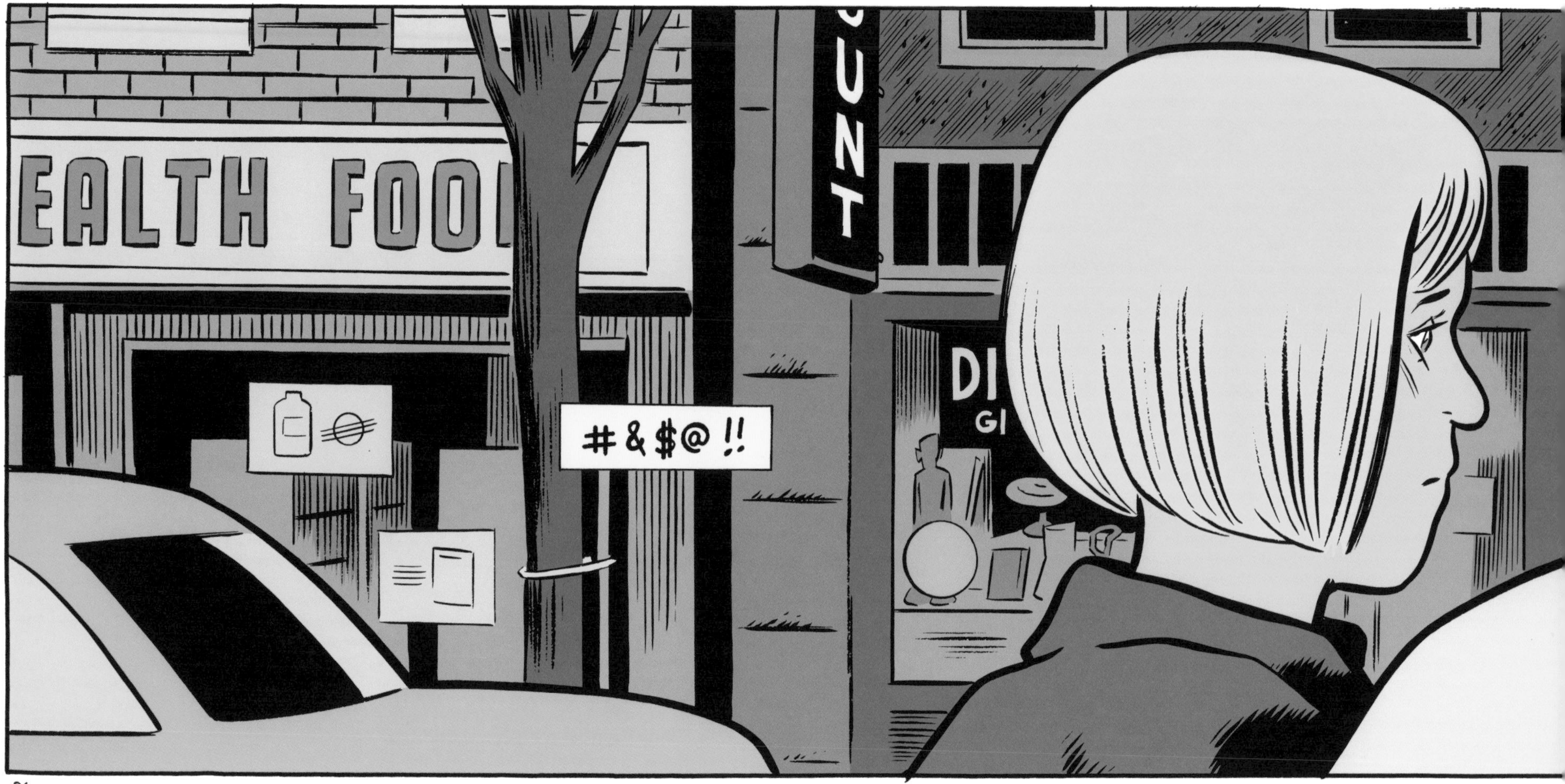
EALTH FOO
UNT
#&$@!!
DI
GI

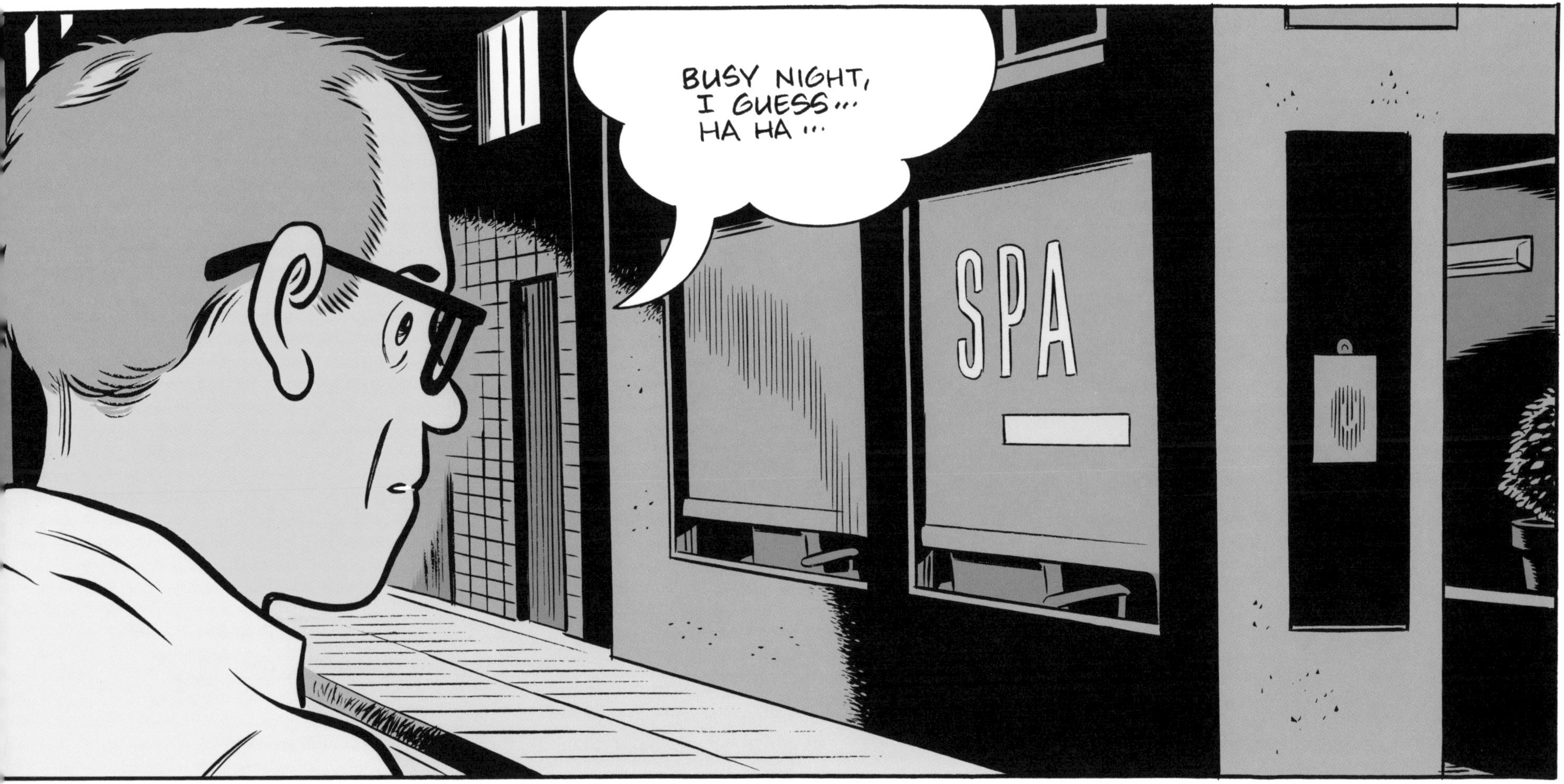
BUSY NIGHT, I GUESS... HA HA...
SPA

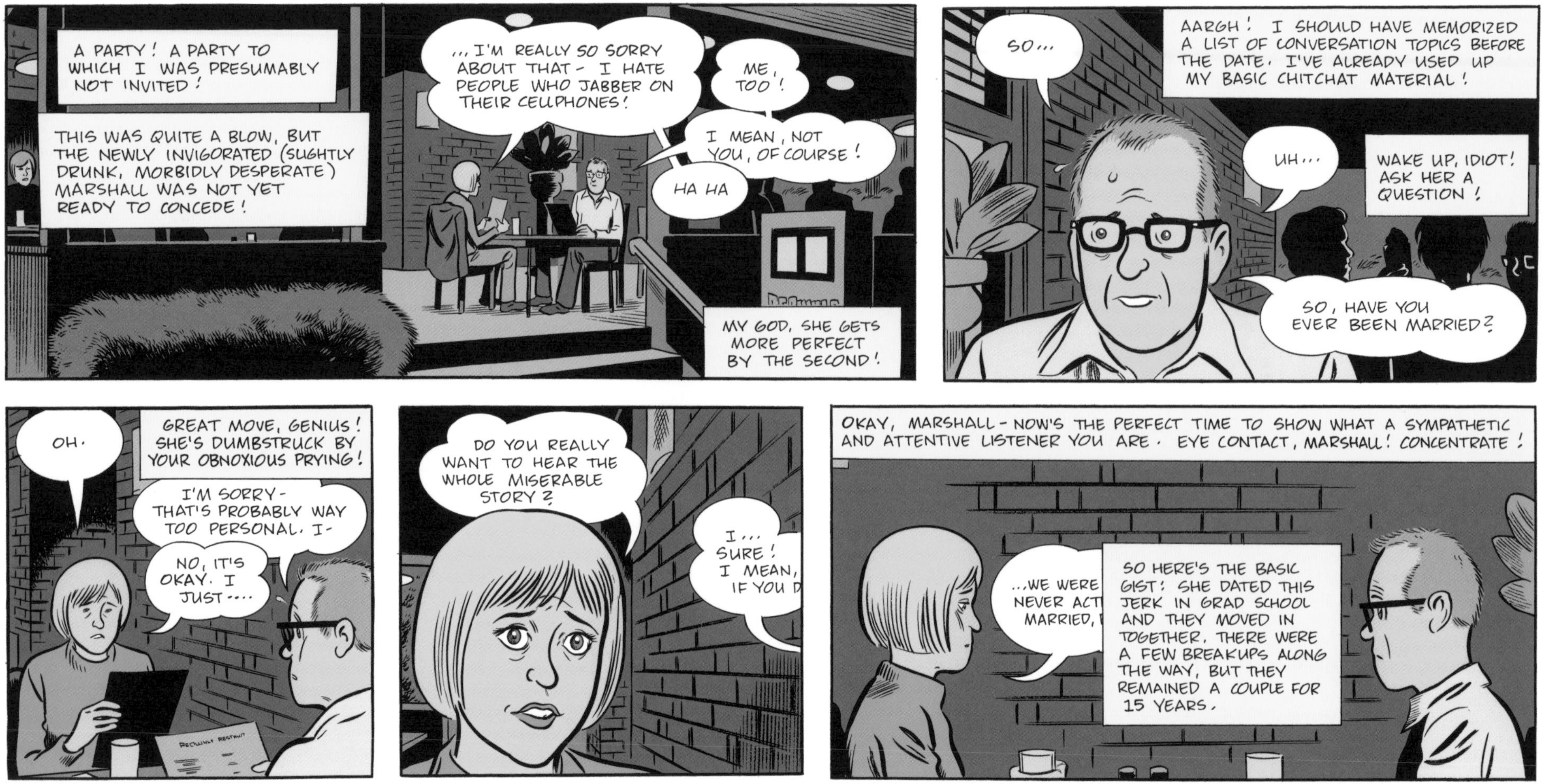
A PARTY! A PARTY TO WHICH I WAS PRESUMABLY NOT INVITED!
THIS WAS QUITE A BLOW, BUT THE NEWLY INVIGORATED (SLIGHTLY DRUNK, MORBIDLY DESPERATE) MARSHALL WAS NOT YET READY TO CONCEDE!
...I'M REALLY SO SORRY ABOUT THAT - I HATE PEOPLE WHO JABBER ON THEIR CELLPHONES!
ME, TOO!
I MEAN, NOT YOU, OF COURSE!
HA HA
MY GOD, SHE GETS MORE PERFECT BY THE SECOND!
SO...
AARGH! I SHOULD HAVE MEMORIZED A LIST OF CONVERSATION TOPICS BEFORE THE DATE. I'VE ALREADY USED UP MY BASIC CHITCHAT MATERIAL!
UH...
WAKE UP, IDIOT! ASK HER A QUESTION!
SO, HAVE YOU EVER BEEN MARRIED?
OH.
GREAT MOVE, GENIUS! SHE'S DUMBSTRUCK BY YOUR OBNOXIOUS PRYING!
I'M SORRY - THAT'S PROBABLY WAY TOO PERSONAL. I-
NO, IT'S OKAY. I JUST....
DO YOU REALLY WANT TO HEAR THE WHOLE MISERABLE STORY?
I... SURE! I MEAN, IF YOU
OKAY, MARSHALL - NOW'S THE PERFECT TIME TO SHOW WHAT A SYMPATHETIC AND ATTENTIVE LISTENER YOU ARE. EYE CONTACT, MARSHALL! CONCENTRATE!
...WE WERE NEVER ACT MARRIED,
SO HERE'S THE BASIC GIST: SHE DATED THIS JERK IN GRAD SCHOOL AND THEY MOVED IN TOGETHER. THERE WERE A FEW BREAKUPS ALONG THE WAY, BUT THEY REMAINED A COUPLE FOR 15 YEARS.

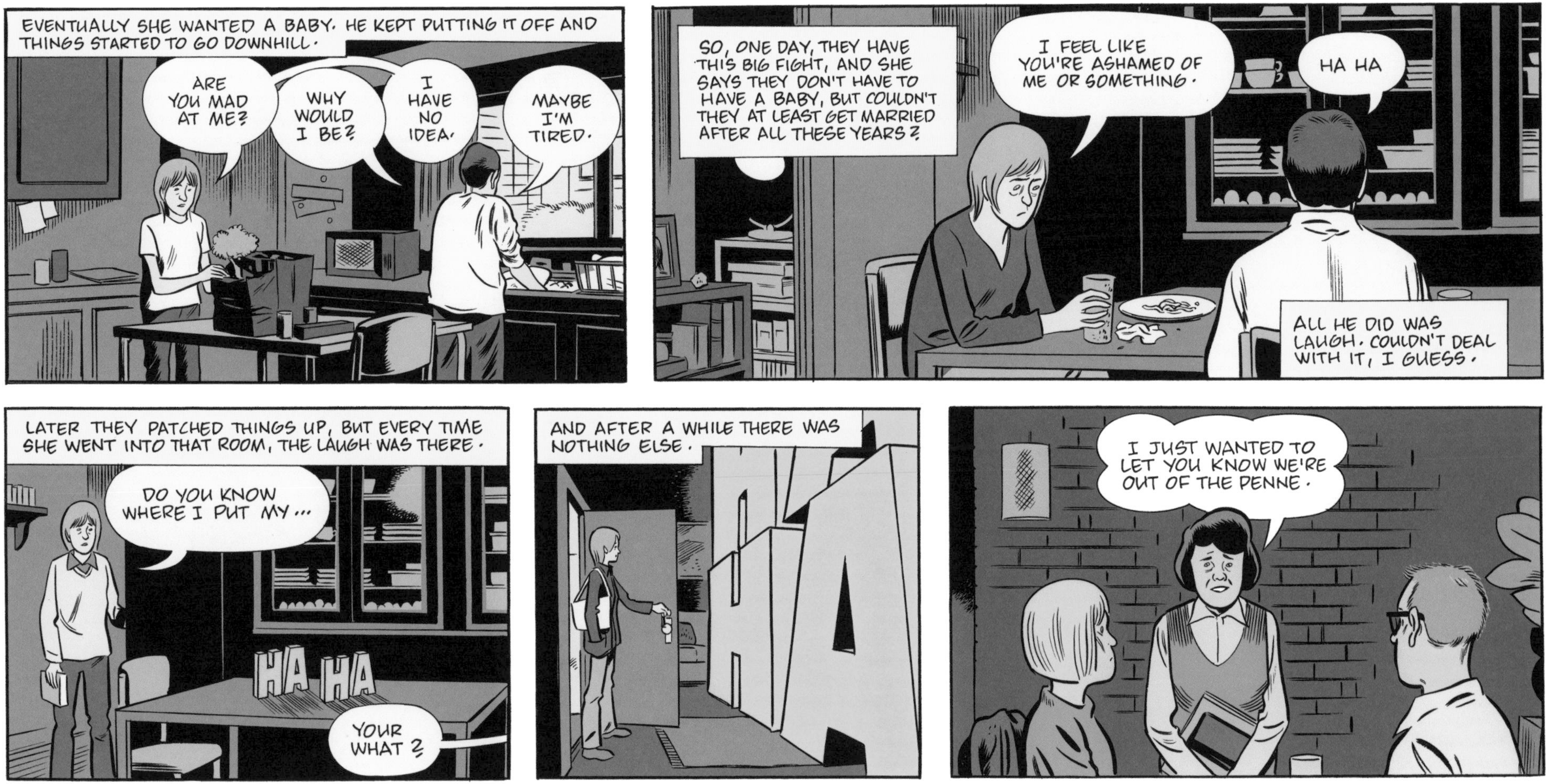

EVENTUALLY SHE WANTED A BABY. HE KEPT PUTTING IT OFF AND THINGS STARTED TO GO DOWNHILL.
ARE YOU MAD AT ME?
WHY WOULD I BE?
I HAVE NO IDEA.
MAYBE I'M TIRED.
SO, ONE DAY, THEY HAVE THIS BIG FIGHT, AND SHE SAYS THEY DON'T HAVE TO HAVE A BABY, BUT COULDN'T THEY AT LEAST GET MARRIED AFTER ALL THESE YEARS?
I FEEL LIKE YOU'RE ASHAMED OF ME OR SOMETHING.
HA HA
ALL HE DID WAS LAUGH. COULDN'T DEAL WITH IT, I GUESS.
LATER THEY PATCHED THINGS UP, BUT EVERY TIME SHE WENT INTO THAT ROOM, THE LAUGH WAS THERE.
DO YOU KNOW WHERE I PUT MY...
HA HA
YOUR WHAT?
AND AFTER A WHILE THERE WAS NOTHING ELSE.
HA
I JUST WANTED TO LET YOU KNOW WE'RE OUT OF THE PENNE.

WHEN TIM TOLD ME SHE WAS "ONE OF A KIND," I THOUGHT HE WAS JUST TRYING TO SELL ME ON THE WHOLE BLIND-DATE CONCEPT. I SHOULD HAVE TAKEN HIM AT HIS WORD; SHE'S A MIRACLE!

AND NOW, WITH HER OWN TRAGIC STORY DRAWING TO A CLOSE, HERE WAS A CHANCE TO CEMENT OUR BOND IN MUTUAL MISERY WITH MY OWN UNTOPPABLE LEGACY OF ROMANTIC WOE.

YES, I'M AFRAID I KNOW EXACTLY WHAT YOU MEAN. I—

POP!

WHAT THE ?!

SCHMUCK! WHAT ARE YOU DOING?! DON'T BUM HER OUT WITH YOUR SOB SISTER CRAP! WHAT'S WRONG WITH YOU!?

BUT...

TO ME WORST IT WAS HE DI

WHAT ARE YOU GONNA SAY? "HI, I'M A BIG CRYBABY LOSER WHO DIDN'T GO ON A DATE FOR SIX YEARS UNTIL I MET A DERANGED HOOKER AND NOW I'M READY FOR SOME SERIOUS LOVIN', BABY!"?

WELL, I....

THAT STUFF DON'T PLAY, BRO'! Y'GOTTA LOOSEN UP ON THE FACTS — MAKE HER THINK YOU'RE NOT THE UTTERLY UNWANTED LITTLE NOTHING YOU REALLY ARE!

BUT SHE'S DIFFERENT. I CAN BE HONEST WITH HER.....

NOBODY'S DIFFERENT!

REMEMBER THE OLD DAYS, BACK WHEN YOU MET THE MISSUS? YOU USED TO BE ABLE TO **BRING IT!**

BUT I DON'T WANT TO LIE. I WANT HER TO KNOW THE REAL—

OH, PLEASE!

WHAT "LIE"? YOU'RE KEEPING PERSONAL STUFF TO YOURSELF, THAT'S ALL! WHAT'S THIS BIG COMPULSION TO SPILL THE BEANS?

I JUST—

SHUSH!

CAN I AT LEAST TELL HER I WAS MARRIED?

SAVE IT FOR THE HONEYMOON! TELL HER YOU'RE A "SUCCESSFUL SELF-EMPLOYED BACHELOR WHO'S TIRED OF PLAYING THE FIELD."

"SUCCESSFUL"? I CAN'T EVEN AFFORD TO PAY FOR THIS DINNER! UNLESS SOMETHING COMES ALONG BY THE END OF THE MONTH, I'LL BE LIVING IN MY CAR!

LOOK, I GET THAT YOU'RE A LOSER — I'M JUST SAYIN', BEST TO TAKE IT ONE STEP AT A TIME.

BUT WHAT HAPPENS WHEN SHE FINDS OUT THE TRUTH? I CAN'T JUST—

JEEZUS! FORGET I SAID ANYTHING!

POP

GOD, LISTEN TO ME — YAMMERING LIKE AN IDIOT ABOUT MY STUPID EX. SHUT UP, NATALIE!

31.

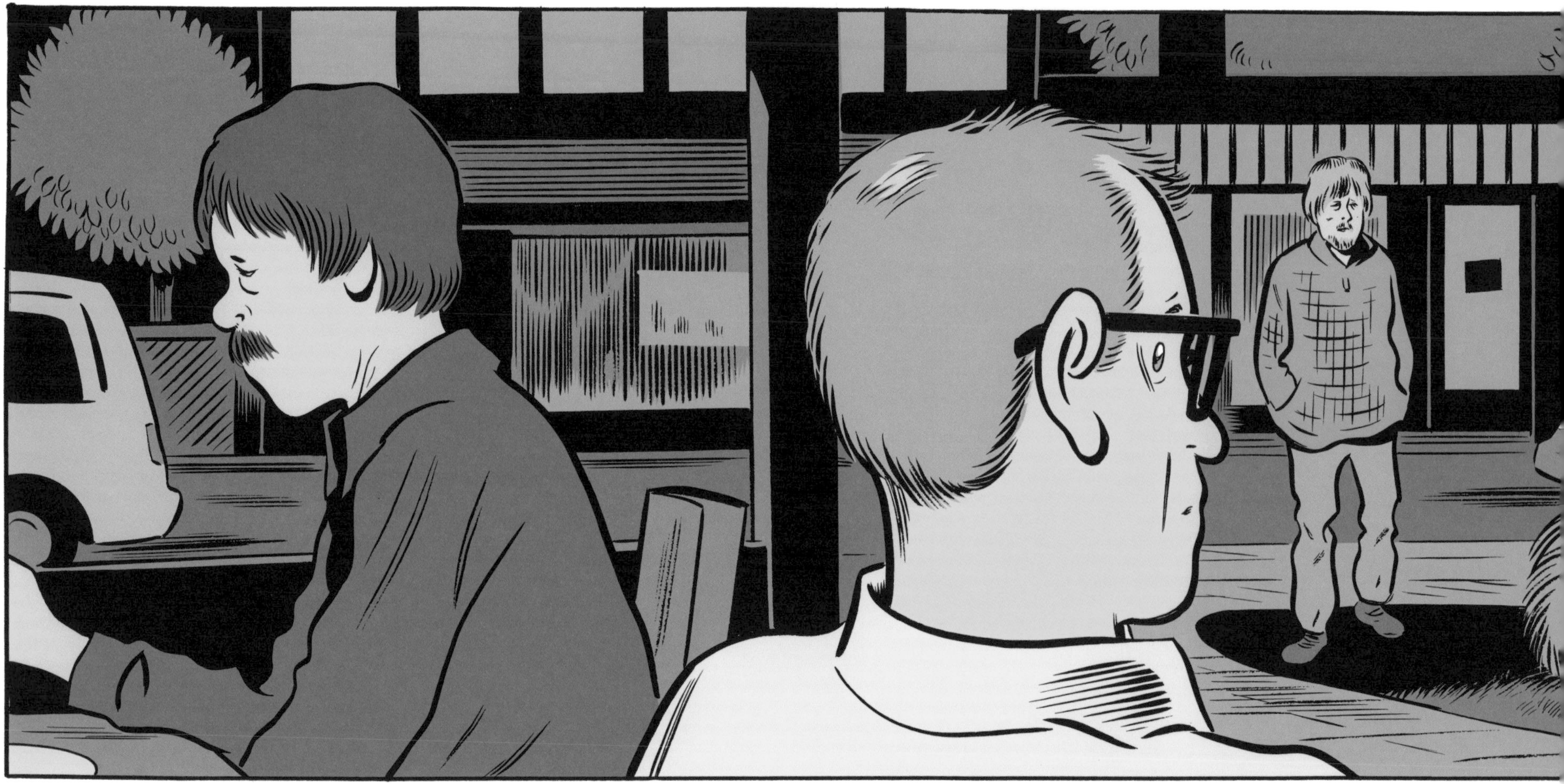

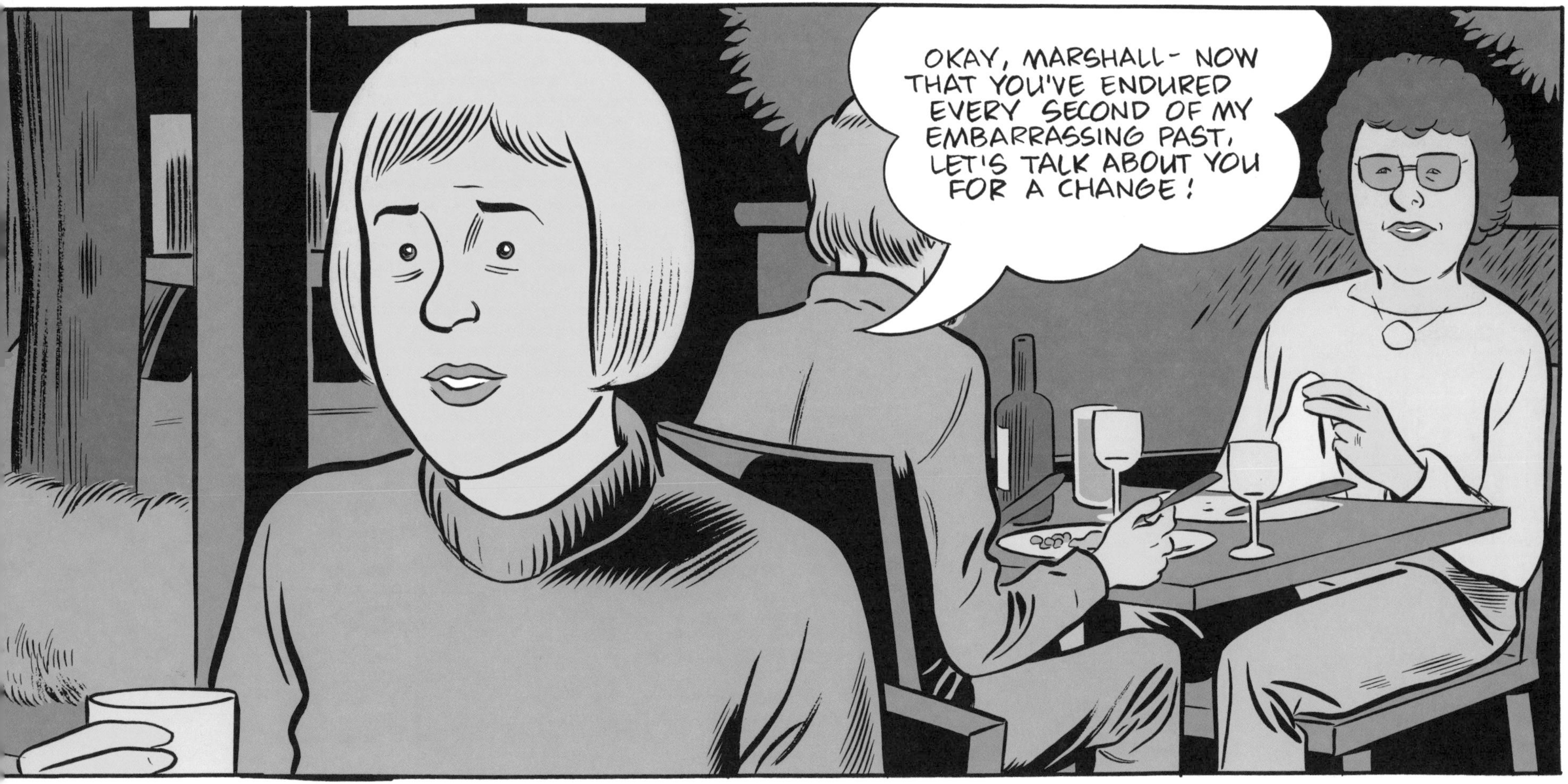
OKAY, MARSHALL- NOW THAT YOU'VE ENDURED EVERY SECOND OF MY EMBARRASSING PAST, LET'S TALK ABOUT YOU FOR A CHANGE!

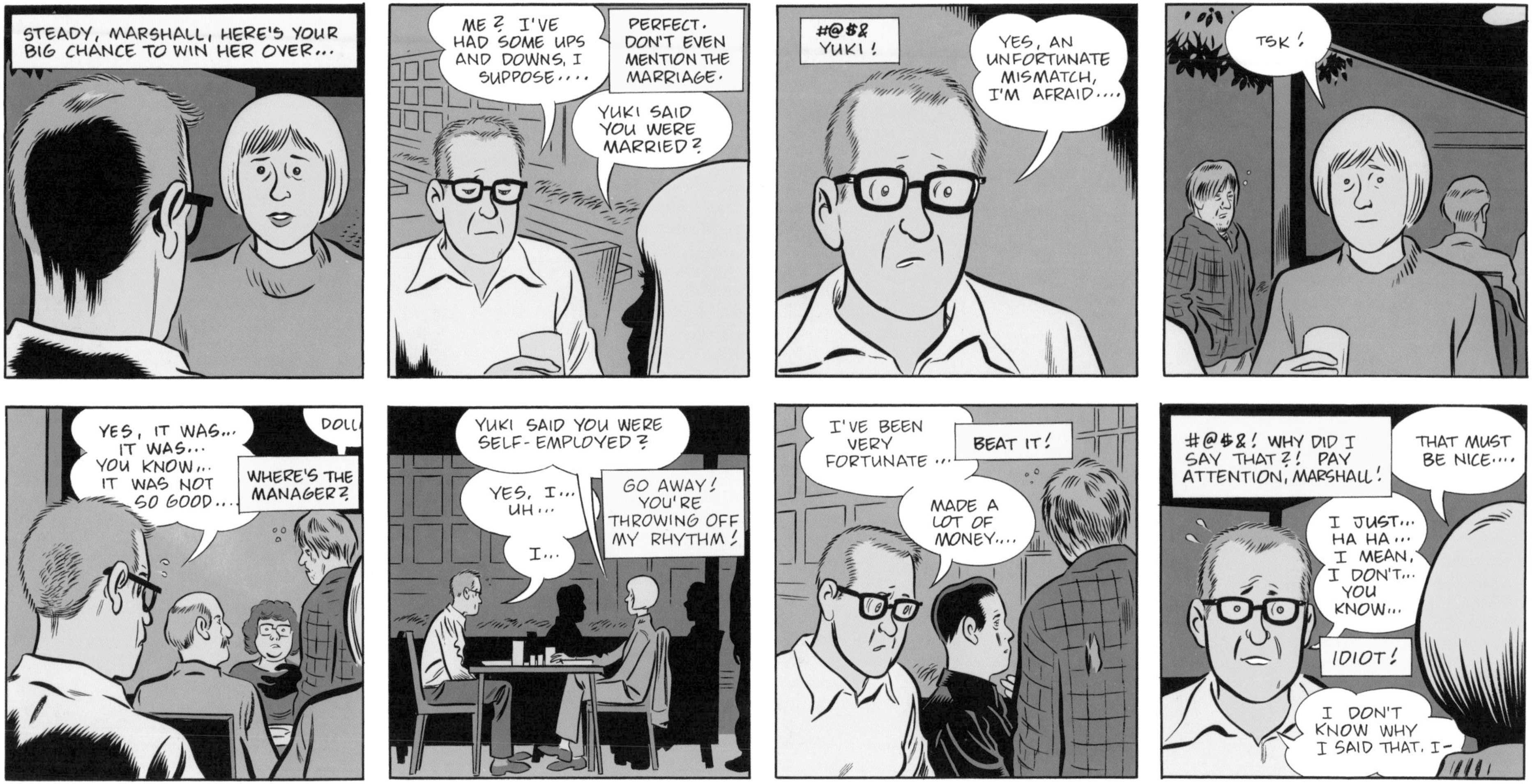
STEADY, MARSHALL, HERE'S YOUR BIG CHANCE TO WIN HER OVER...
ME? I'VE HAD SOME UPS AND DOWNS, I SUPPOSE....
PERFECT. DON'T EVEN MENTION THE MARRIAGE.
YUKI SAID YOU WERE MARRIED?
#@$& YUKI!
YES, AN UNFORTUNATE MISMATCH, I'M AFRAID....
TSK!
YES, IT WAS... IT WAS... YOU KNOW... IT WAS NOT SO GOOD....
WHERE'S THE MANAGER?
YUKI SAID YOU WERE SELF-EMPLOYED?
YES, I... UH...
I...
GO AWAY! YOU'RE THROWING OFF MY RHYTHM!
I'VE BEEN VERY FORTUNATE ...
BEAT IT!
MADE A LOT OF MONEY....
#@$&! WHY DID I SAY THAT?! PAY ATTENTION, MARSHALL!
THAT MUST BE NICE....
I JUST... HA HA... I MEAN, I DON'T... YOU KNOW...
IDIOT!
I DON'T KNOW WHY I SAID THAT. I-

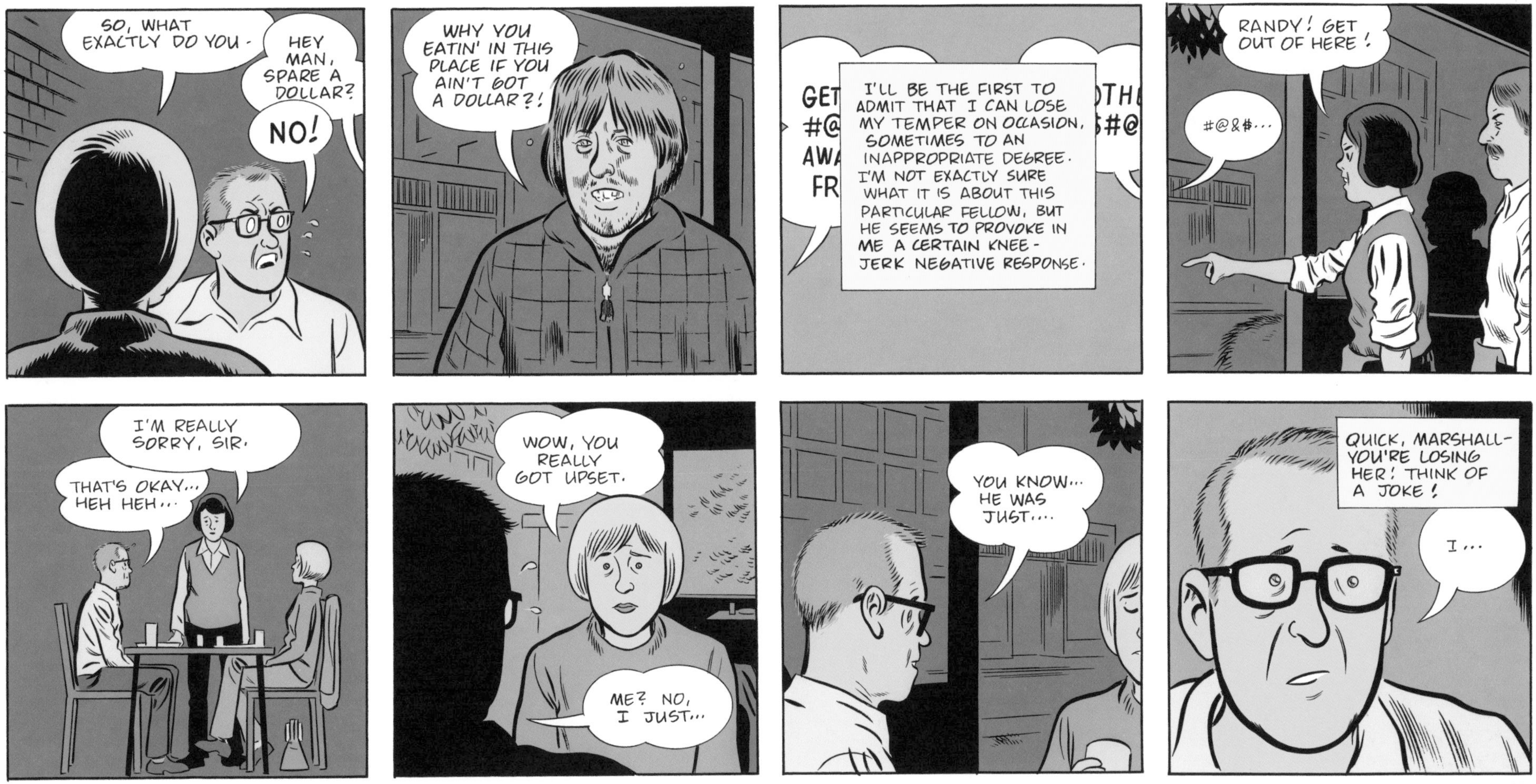
SO, WHAT EXACTLY DO YOU -
HEY MAN, SPARE A DOLLAR?
NO!
WHY YOU EATIN' IN THIS PLACE IF YOU AIN'T GOT A DOLLAR?!
I'LL BE THE FIRST TO ADMIT THAT I CAN LOSE MY TEMPER ON OCCASION, SOMETIMES TO AN INAPPROPRIATE DEGREE. I'M NOT EXACTLY SURE WHAT IT IS ABOUT THIS PARTICULAR FELLOW, BUT HE SEEMS TO PROVOKE IN ME A CERTAIN KNEE-JERK NEGATIVE RESPONSE.
RANDY! GET OUT OF HERE!
#@&#...
I'M REALLY SORRY, SIR.
THAT'S OKAY... HEH HEH...
WOW, YOU REALLY GOT UPSET.
ME? NO, I JUST...
YOU KNOW... HE WAS JUST....
QUICK, MARSHALL- YOU'RE LOSING HER! THINK OF A JOKE!
I...

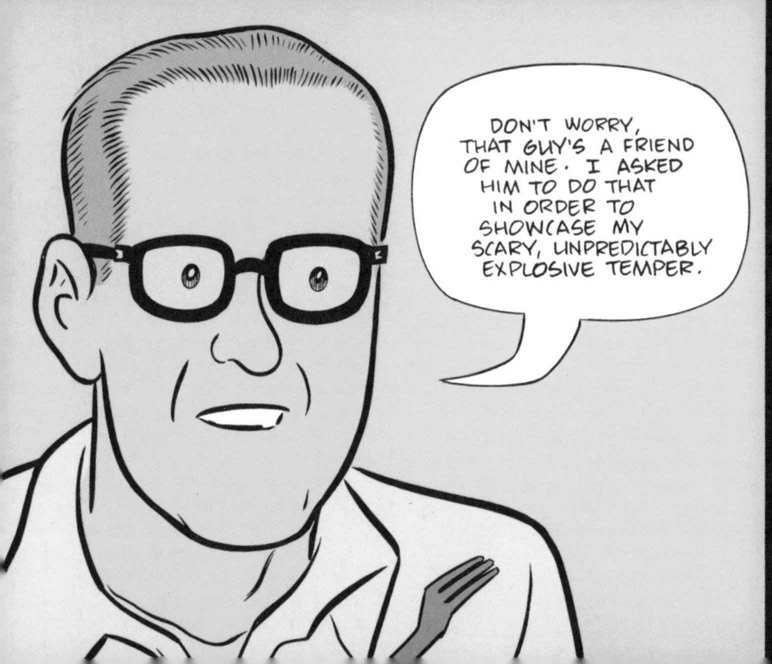
DON'T WORRY, THAT GUY'S A FRIEND OF MINE. I ASKED HIM TO DO THAT IN ORDER TO SHOWCASE MY SCARY, UNPREDICTABLY EXPLOSIVE TEMPER.

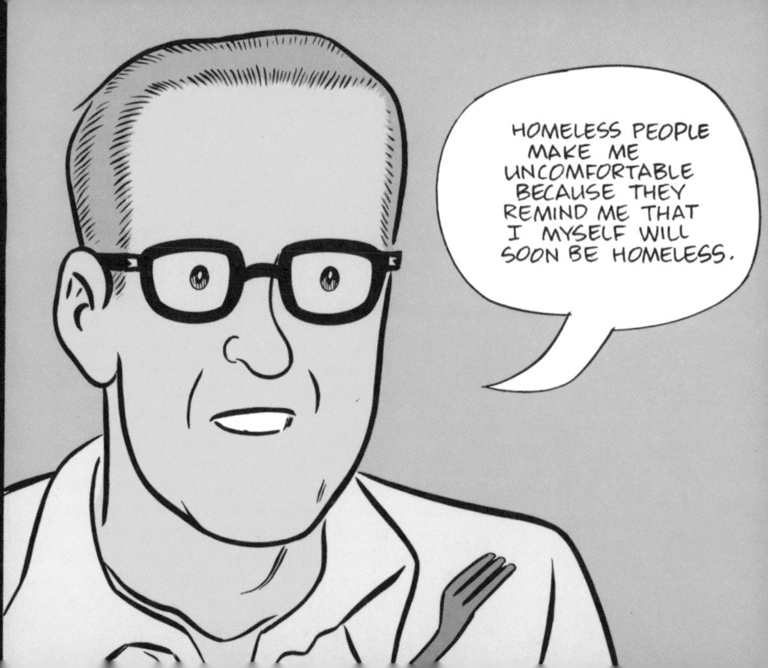
HOMELESS PEOPLE MAKE ME UNCOMFORTABLE BECAUSE THEY REMIND ME THAT I MYSELF WILL SOON BE HOMELESS.

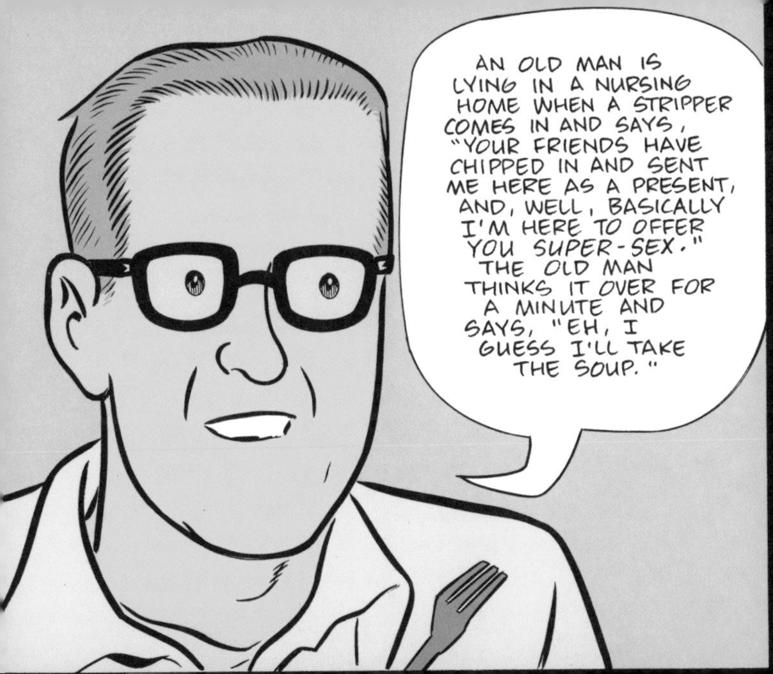
AN OLD MAN IS LYING IN A NURSING HOME WHEN A STRIPPER COMES IN AND SAYS, "YOUR FRIENDS HAVE CHIPPED IN AND SENT ME HERE AS A PRESENT, AND, WELL, BASICALLY I'M HERE TO OFFER YOU SUPER-SEX." THE OLD MAN THINKS IT OVER FOR A MINUTE AND SAYS, "EH, I GUESS I'LL TAKE THE SOUP."

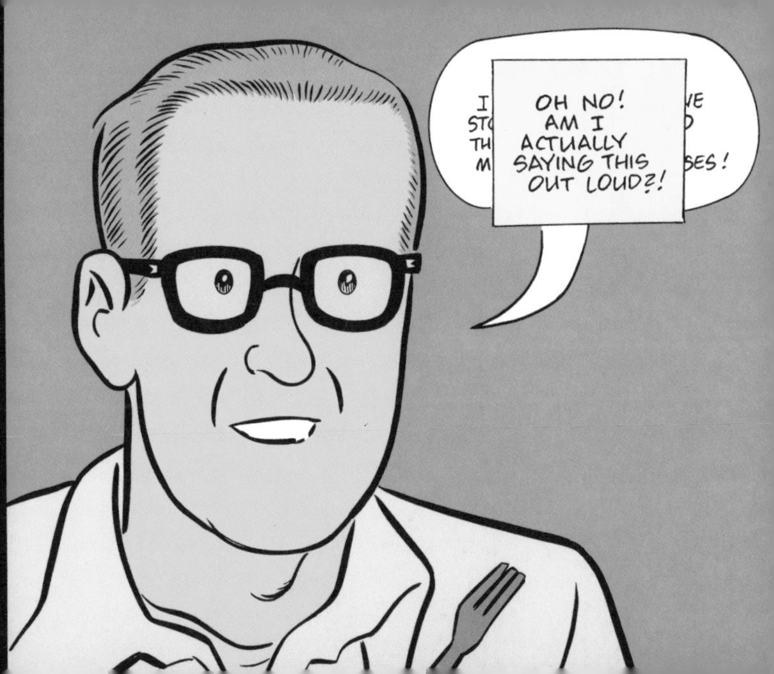
OH NO! AM I ACTUALLY SAYING THIS OUT LOUD?!

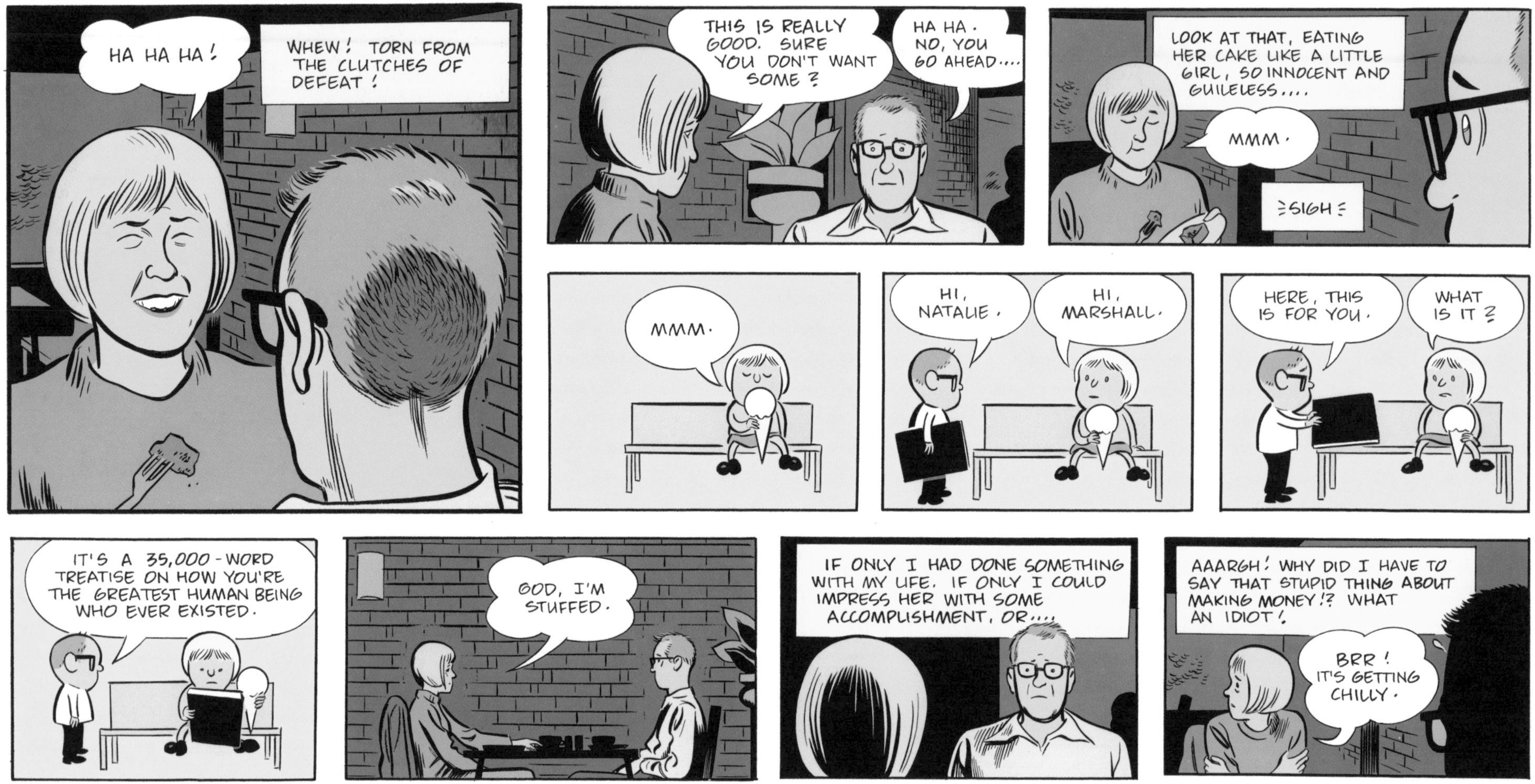
HA HA HA!
WHEW! TORN FROM THE CLUTCHES OF DEFEAT!
THIS IS REALLY GOOD. SURE YOU DON'T WANT SOME?
HA HA. NO, YOU GO AHEAD....
LOOK AT THAT, EATING HER CAKE LIKE A LITTLE GIRL, SO INNOCENT AND GUILELESS....
MMM.
SIGH
MMM.
HI, NATALIE.
HI, MARSHALL.
HERE, THIS IS FOR YOU.
WHAT IS IT?
IT'S A 35,000-WORD TREATISE ON HOW YOU'RE THE GREATEST HUMAN BEING WHO EVER EXISTED.
GOD, I'M STUFFED.
IF ONLY I HAD DONE SOMETHING WITH MY LIFE. IF ONLY I COULD IMPRESS HER WITH SOME ACCOMPLISHMENT, OR....
AAARGH! WHY DID I HAVE TO SAY THAT STUPID THING ABOUT MAKING MONEY!? WHAT AN IDIOT!
BRR! IT'S GETTING CHILLY.

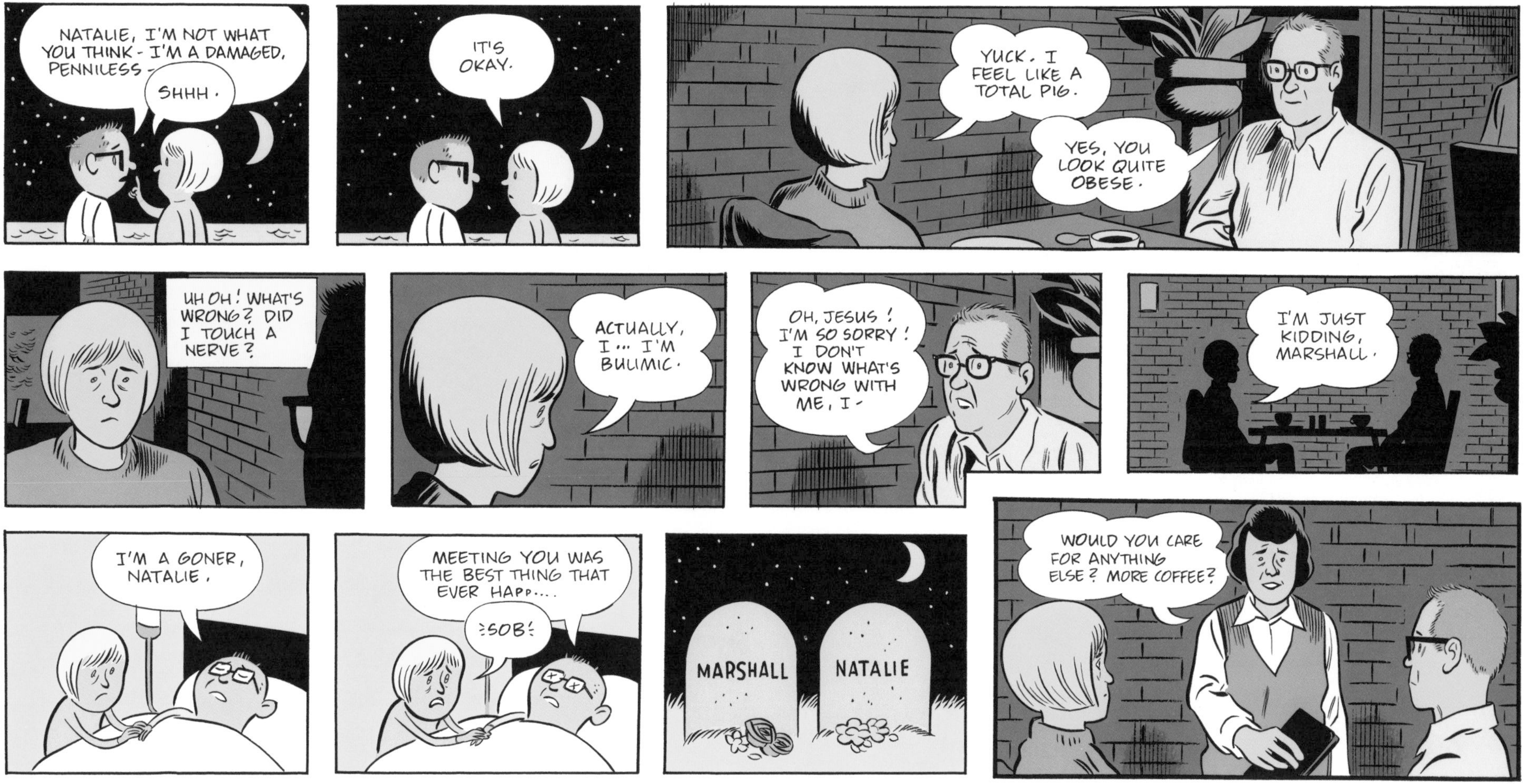
NATALIE, I'M NOT WHAT YOU THINK - I'M A DAMAGED, PENNILESS -
SHHH.
IT'S OKAY.
YUCK. I FEEL LIKE A TOTAL PIG.
YES, YOU LOOK QUITE OBESE.
UH OH! WHAT'S WRONG? DID I TOUCH A NERVE?
ACTUALLY, I... I'M BULIMIC.
OH, JESUS! I'M SO SORRY! I DON'T KNOW WHAT'S WRONG WITH ME, I -
I'M JUST KIDDING, MARSHALL.
I'M A GONER, NATALIE.
MEETING YOU WAS THE BEST THING THAT EVER HAPP....
SOB
MARSHALL
NATALIE
WOULD YOU CARE FOR ANYTHING ELSE? MORE COFFEE?

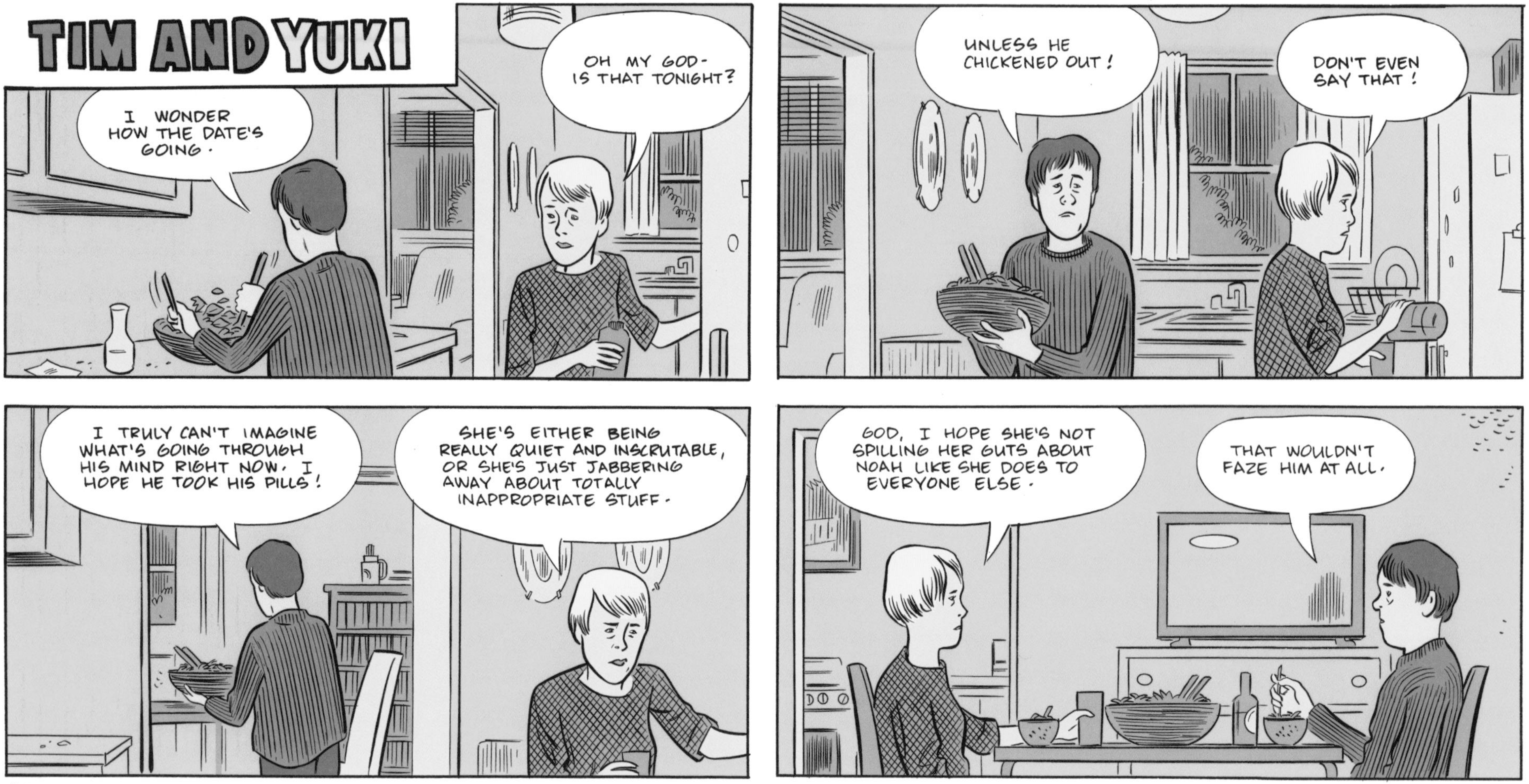
TIM AND YUKI
I WONDER HOW THE DATE'S GOING.
OH MY GOD-IS THAT TONIGHT?
UNLESS HE CHICKENED OUT!
DON'T EVEN SAY THAT!
I TRULY CAN'T IMAGINE WHAT'S GOING THROUGH HIS MIND RIGHT NOW. I HOPE HE TOOK HIS PILLS!
SHE'S EITHER BEING REALLY QUIET AND INSCRUTABLE, OR SHE'S JUST JABBERING AWAY ABOUT TOTALLY INAPPROPRIATE STUFF.
GOD, I HOPE SHE'S NOT SPILLING HER GUTS ABOUT NOAH LIKE SHE DOES TO EVERYONE ELSE.
THAT WOULDN'T FAZE HIM AT ALL.

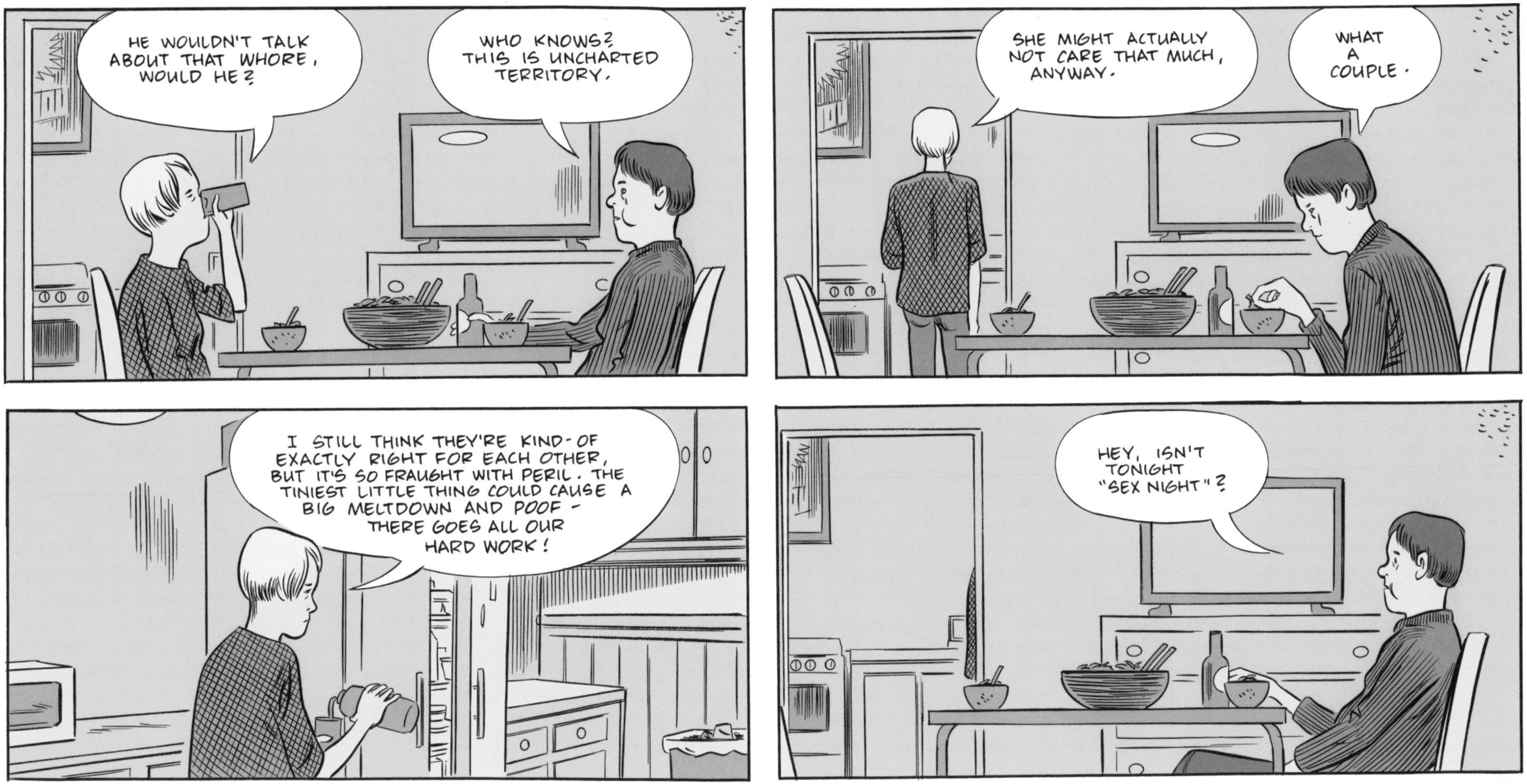
HE WOULDN'T TALK ABOUT THAT WHORE, WOULD HE?
WHO KNOWS? THIS IS UNCHARTED TERRITORY.
SHE MIGHT ACTUALLY NOT CARE THAT MUCH, ANYWAY.
WHAT A COUPLE.
I STILL THINK THEY'RE KIND-OF EXACTLY RIGHT FOR EACH OTHER, BUT IT'S SO FRAUGHT WITH PERIL. THE TINIEST LITTLE THING COULD CAUSE A BIG MELTDOWN AND POOF - THERE GOES ALL OUR HARD WORK!
HEY, ISN'T TONIGHT "SEX NIGHT"?

SO...

TIM AND YUKI OBVIOUSLY KNEW WHAT THEY WERE DOING WHEN THEY SET UP THIS DATE.

CLEARLY, WE'RE PERFECT FOR EACH OTHER.

OR AT LEAST SHE'S PERFECT FOR ME. I WOULD NEVER PRESUME TO...

JESUS, WHY AM I SELF-DEPRECATING EVEN IN MY OWN INTERIOR MONOLOGUE?

I MEAN, IT'S PRETTY CLEAR SHE LIKES ME. SHE PROBABLY HAS JUST AS MUCH RIDING ON THIS AS I DO....

SO, WHAT NOW? DO I TRY TO KISS HER?

SO
MY
I
HE
W

MAYBE THAT'S TOO MUCH. MAYBE I SHOULD SEE IF SHE WANTS TO —

YEAH,
I'M GO
HEAD
WAY,

WAIT A MINUTE — WHAT IS SHE SAYING?

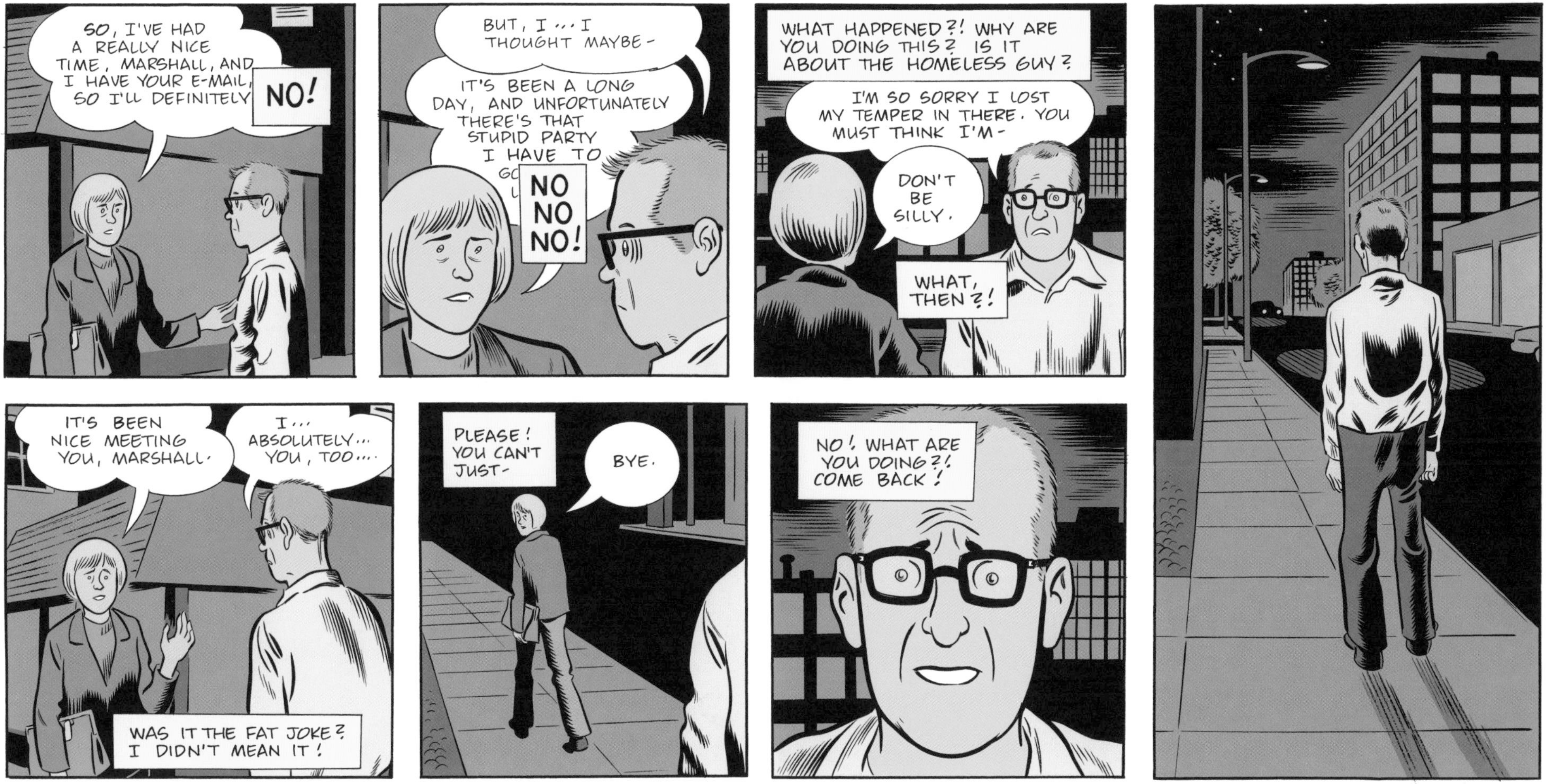
SO, I'VE HAD A REALLY NICE TIME, MARSHALL, AND I HAVE YOUR E-MAIL, SO I'LL DEFINITELY
NO!
BUT, I ... I THOUGHT MAYBE-
IT'S BEEN A LONG DAY, AND UNFORTUNATELY THERE'S THAT STUPID PARTY I HAVE TO
NO NO NO!
WHAT HAPPENED?! WHY ARE YOU DOING THIS? IS IT ABOUT THE HOMELESS GUY?
I'M SO SORRY I LOST MY TEMPER IN THERE. YOU MUST THINK I'M-
DON'T BE SILLY.
WHAT, THEN?!
IT'S BEEN NICE MEETING YOU, MARSHALL.
I... ABSOLUTELY... YOU, TOO....
WAS IT THE FAT JOKE? I DIDN'T MEAN IT!
PLEASE! YOU CAN'T JUST-
BYE.
NO! WHAT ARE YOU DOING?! COME BACK!

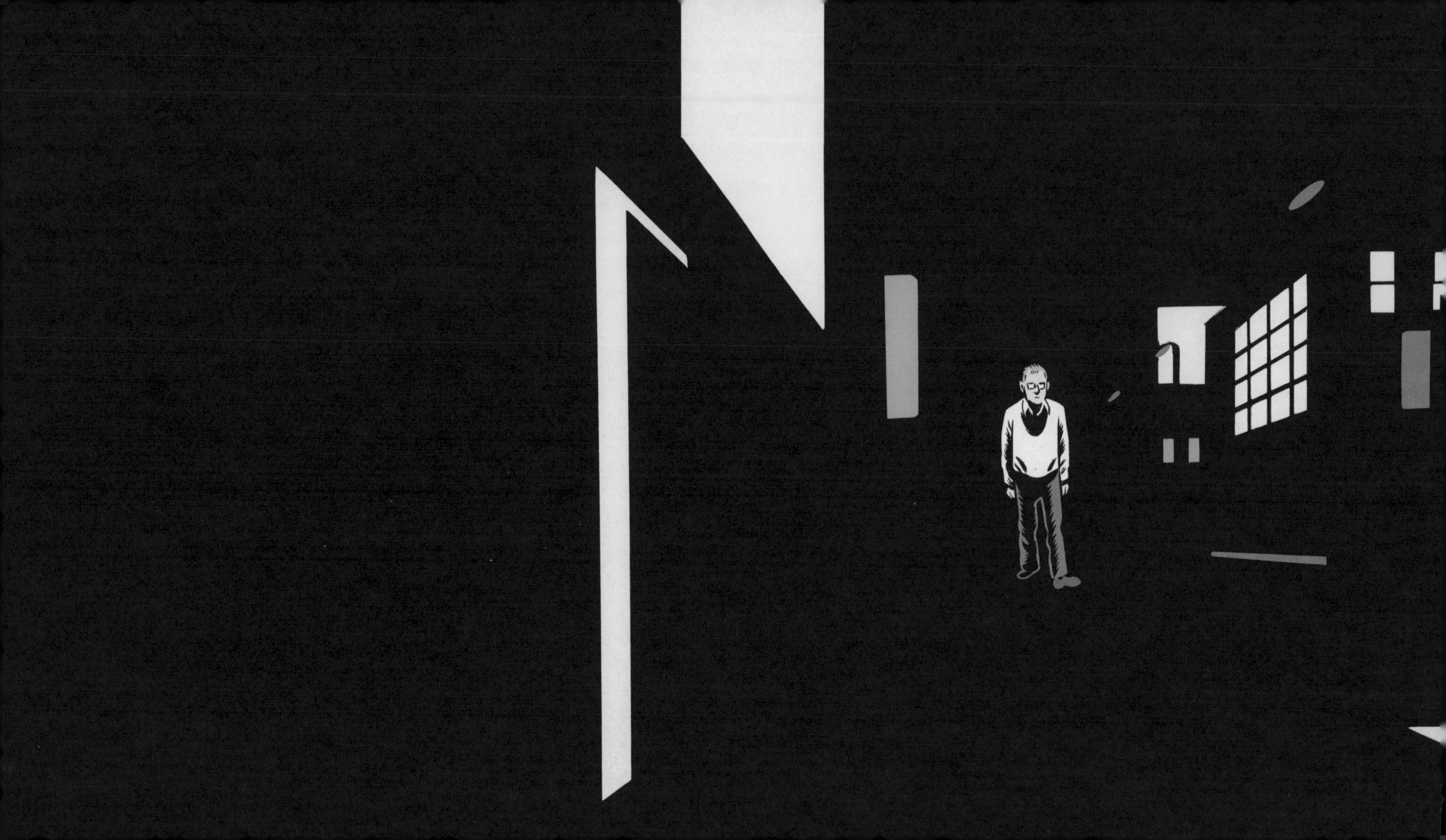

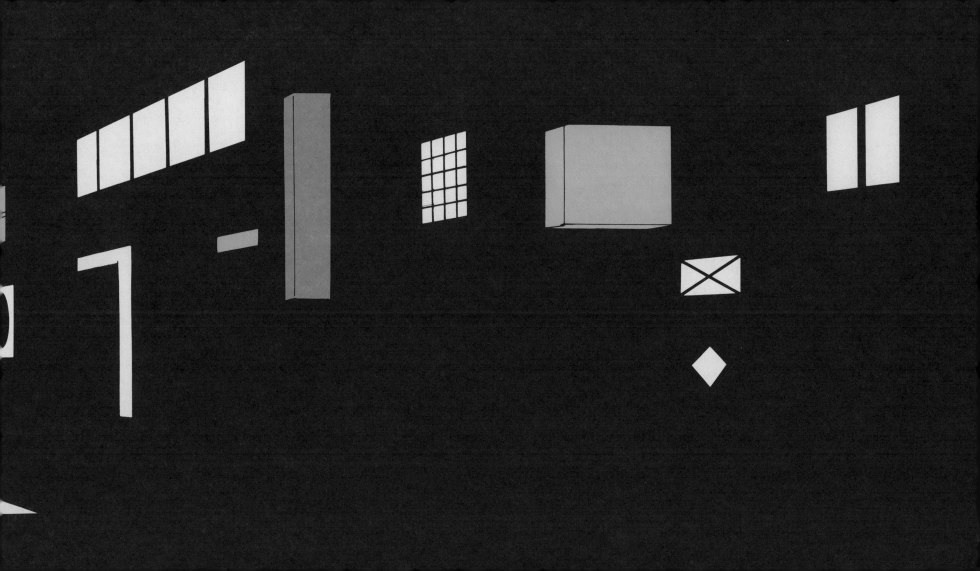

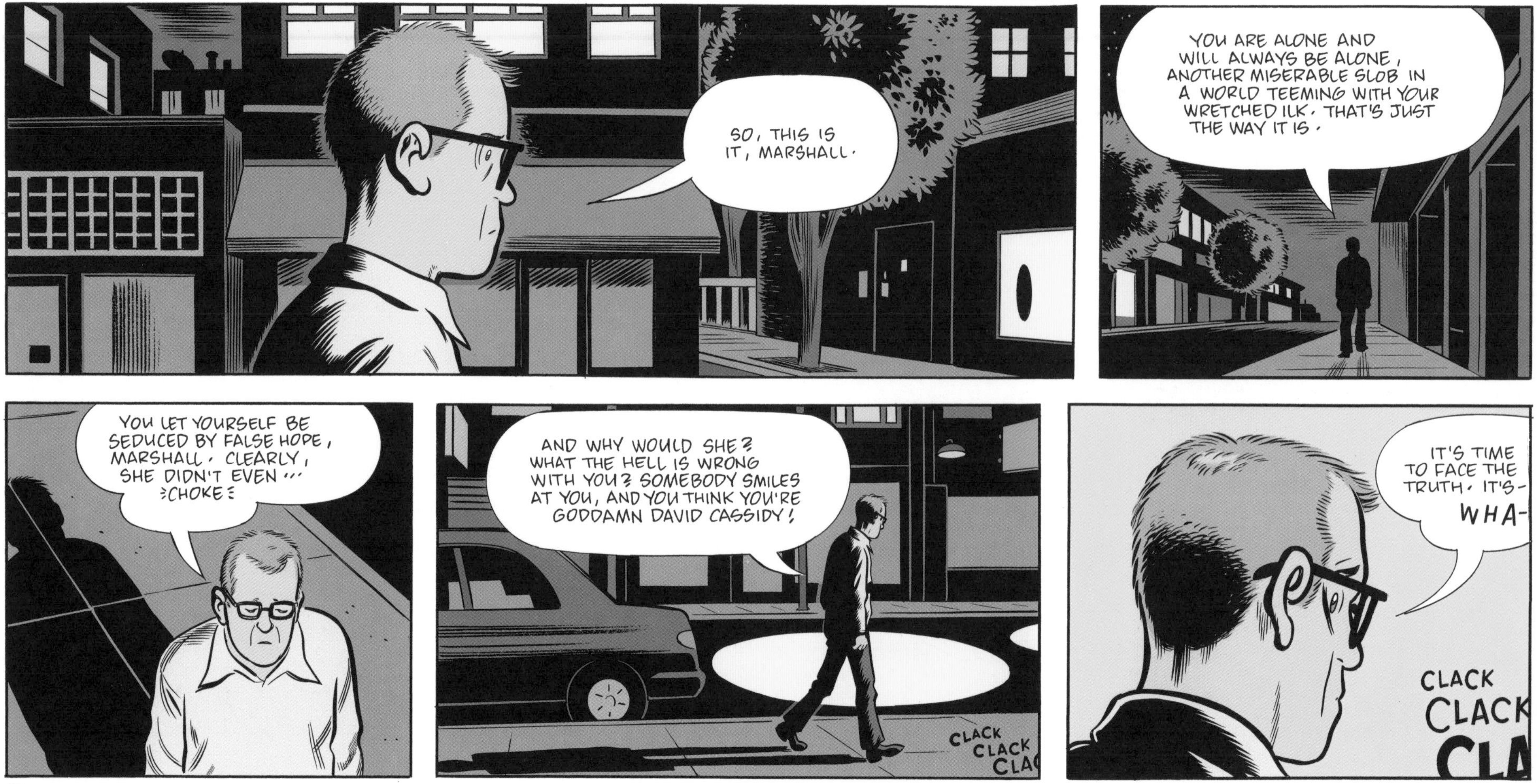
SO, THIS IS IT, MARSHALL.
YOU ARE ALONE AND WILL ALWAYS BE ALONE, ANOTHER MISERABLE SLOB IN A WORLD TEEMING WITH YOUR WRETCHED ILK. THAT'S JUST THE WAY IT IS.
YOU LET YOURSELF BE SEDUCED BY FALSE HOPE, MARSHALL. CLEARLY, SHE DIDN'T EVEN ... ≈CHOKE≈
AND WHY WOULD SHE? WHAT THE HELL IS WRONG WITH YOU? SOMEBODY SMILES AT YOU, AND YOU THINK YOU'RE GODDAMN DAVID CASSIDY!
CLACK CLACK CLAC
IT'S TIME TO FACE THE TRUTH. IT'S-
WHA-
CLACK CLACK CLA

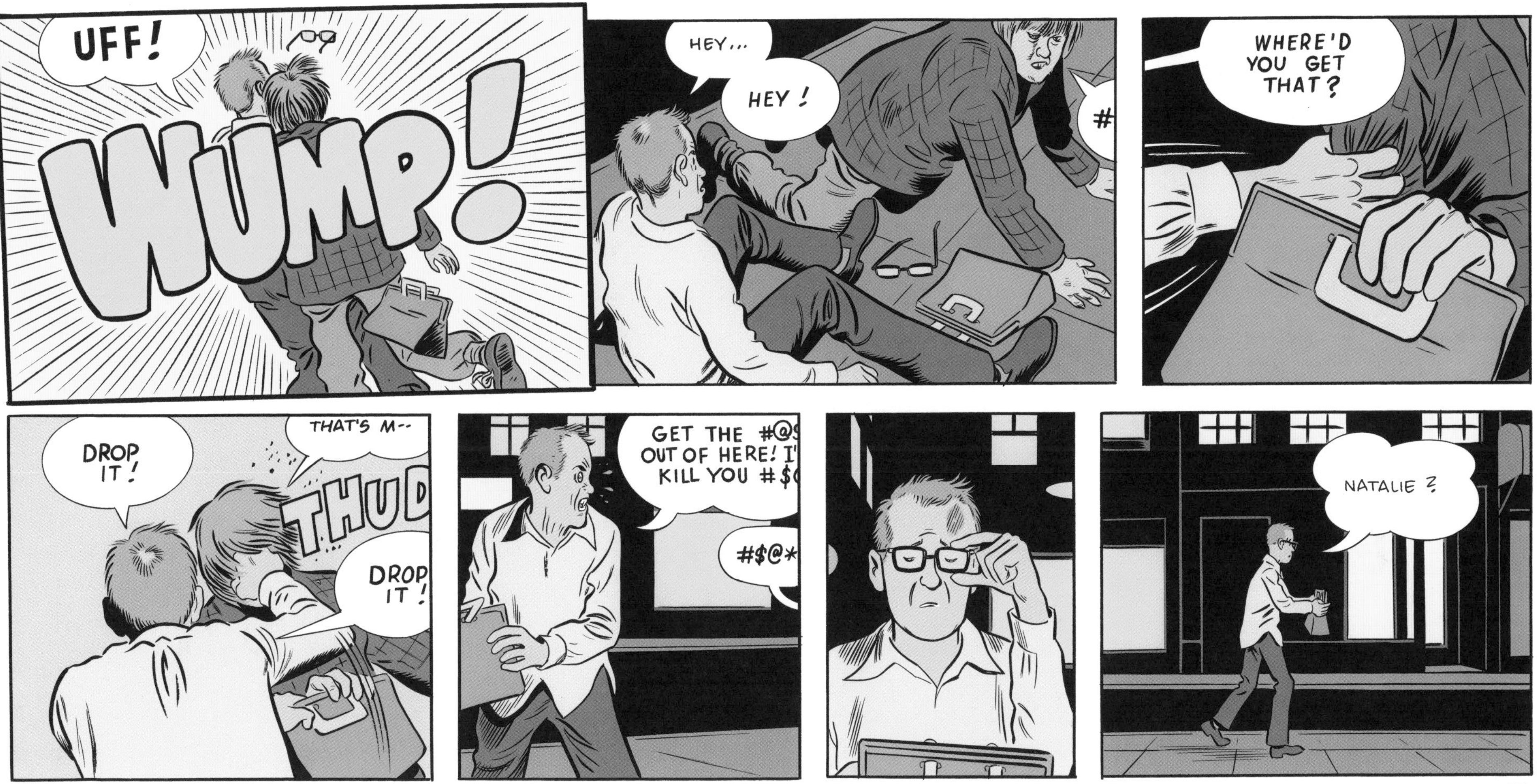
UFF!
WUMP!
HEY...
HEY!
#
WHERE'D YOU GET THAT?
DROP IT!
THAT'S M--
THUD
DROP IT!
GET THE #@$
OUT OF HERE! I'
KILL YOU #$
#$@*
NATALIE?

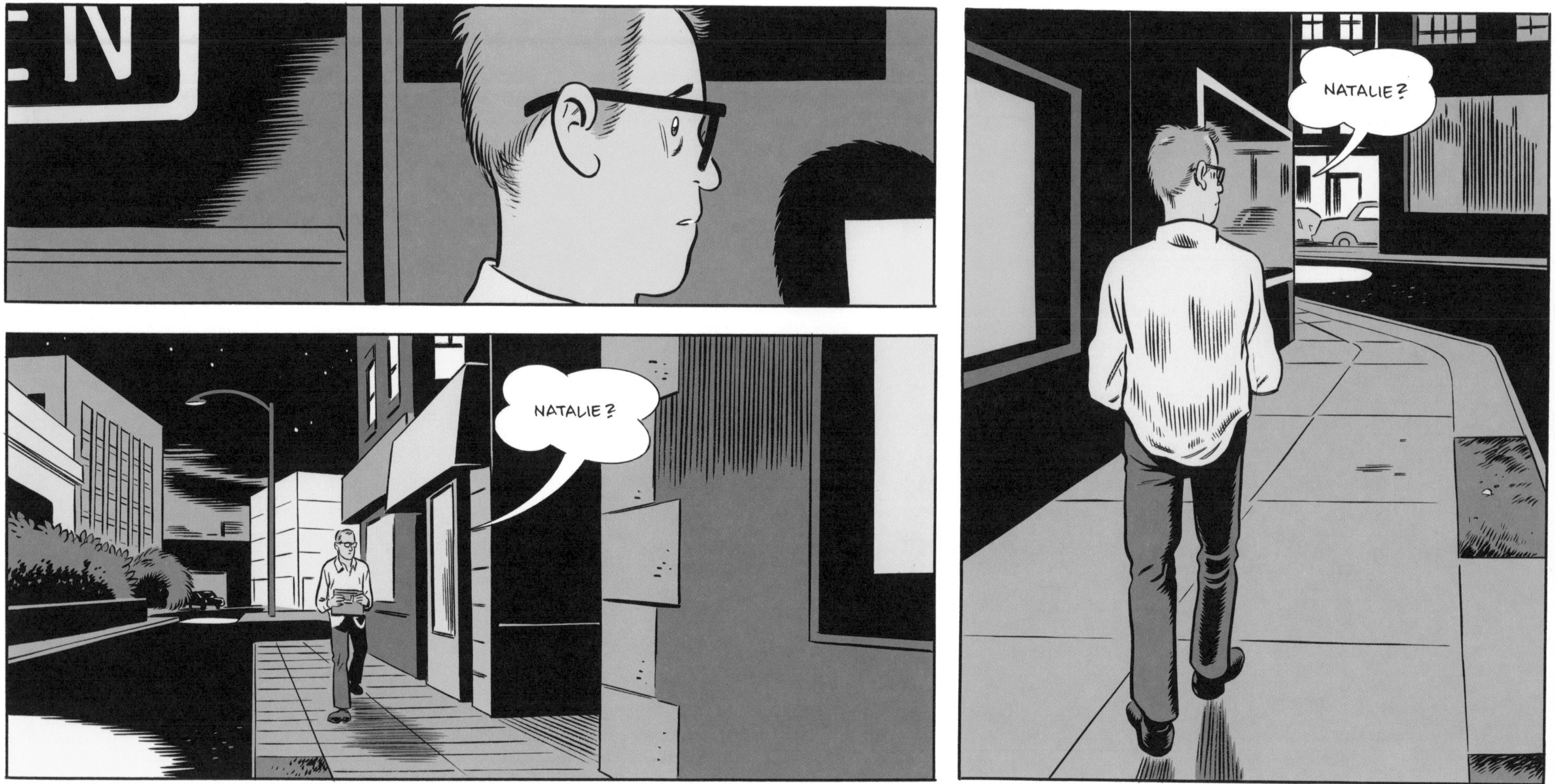
EN
NATALIE?
NATALIE?

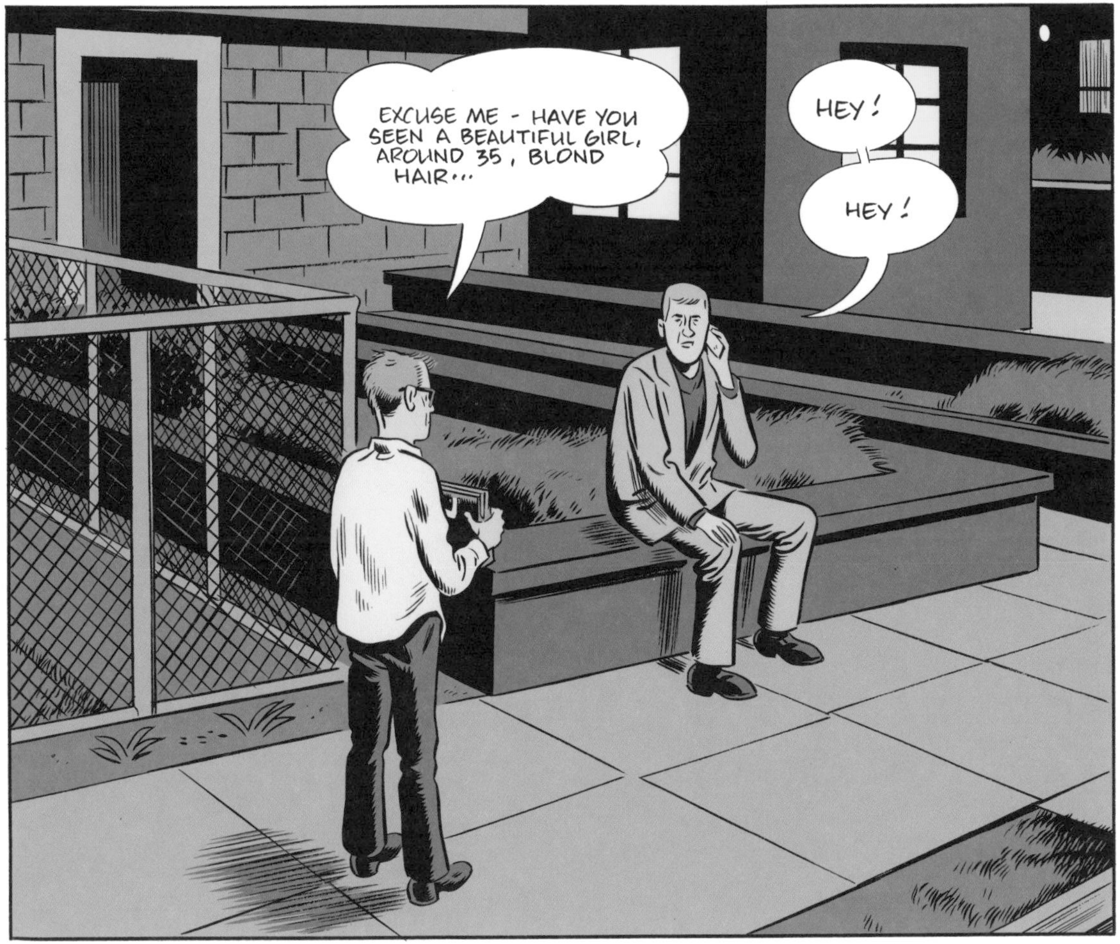
EXCUSE ME - HAVE YOU SEEN A BEAUTIFUL GIRL, AROUND 35, BLOND HAIR...
HEY!
HEY!

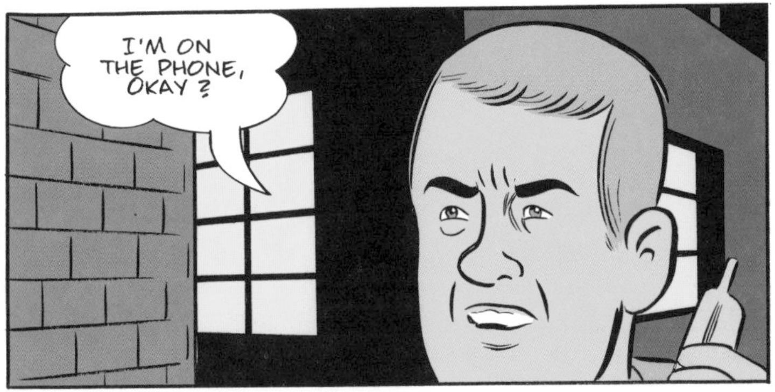
I'M ON THE PHONE, OKAY?

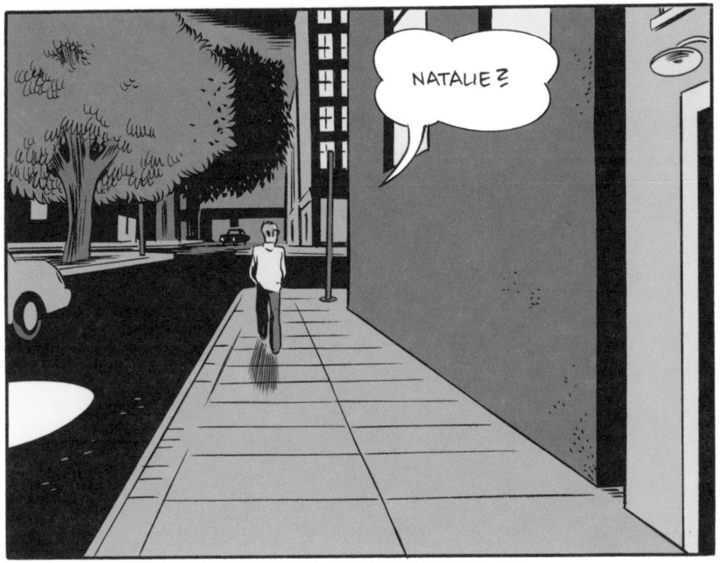
NATALIE?

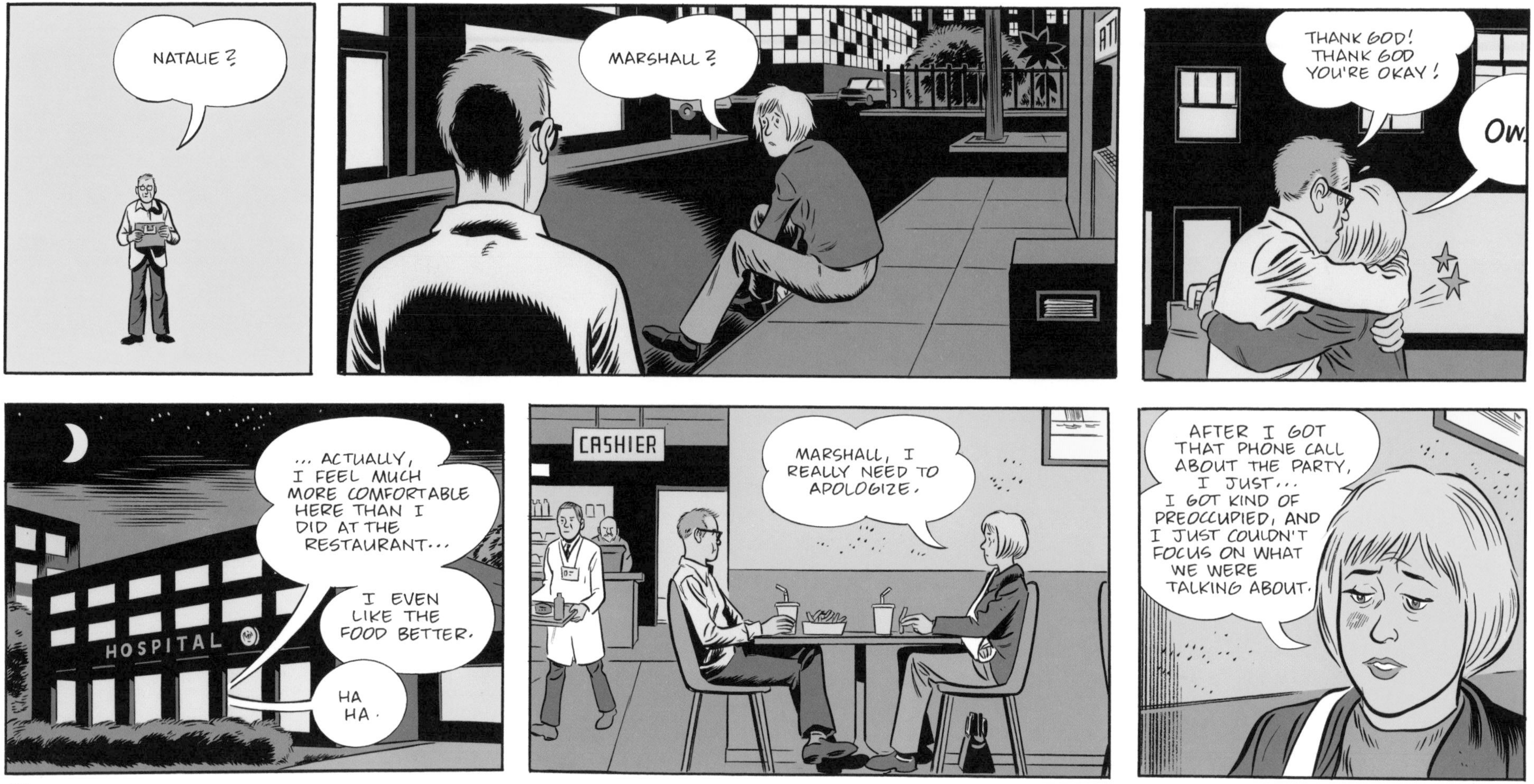
NATALIE?
MARSHALL?
THANK GOD! THANK GOD YOU'RE OKAY!
OW!
... ACTUALLY, I FEEL MUCH MORE COMFORTABLE HERE THAN I DID AT THE RESTAURANT...
I EVEN LIKE THE FOOD BETTER.
HA HA.
HOSPITAL
CASHIER
MARSHALL, I REALLY NEED TO APOLOGIZE.
AFTER I GOT THAT PHONE CALL ABOUT THE PARTY, I JUST... I GOT KIND OF PREOCCUPIED, AND I JUST COULDN'T FOCUS ON WHAT WE WERE TALKING ABOUT.

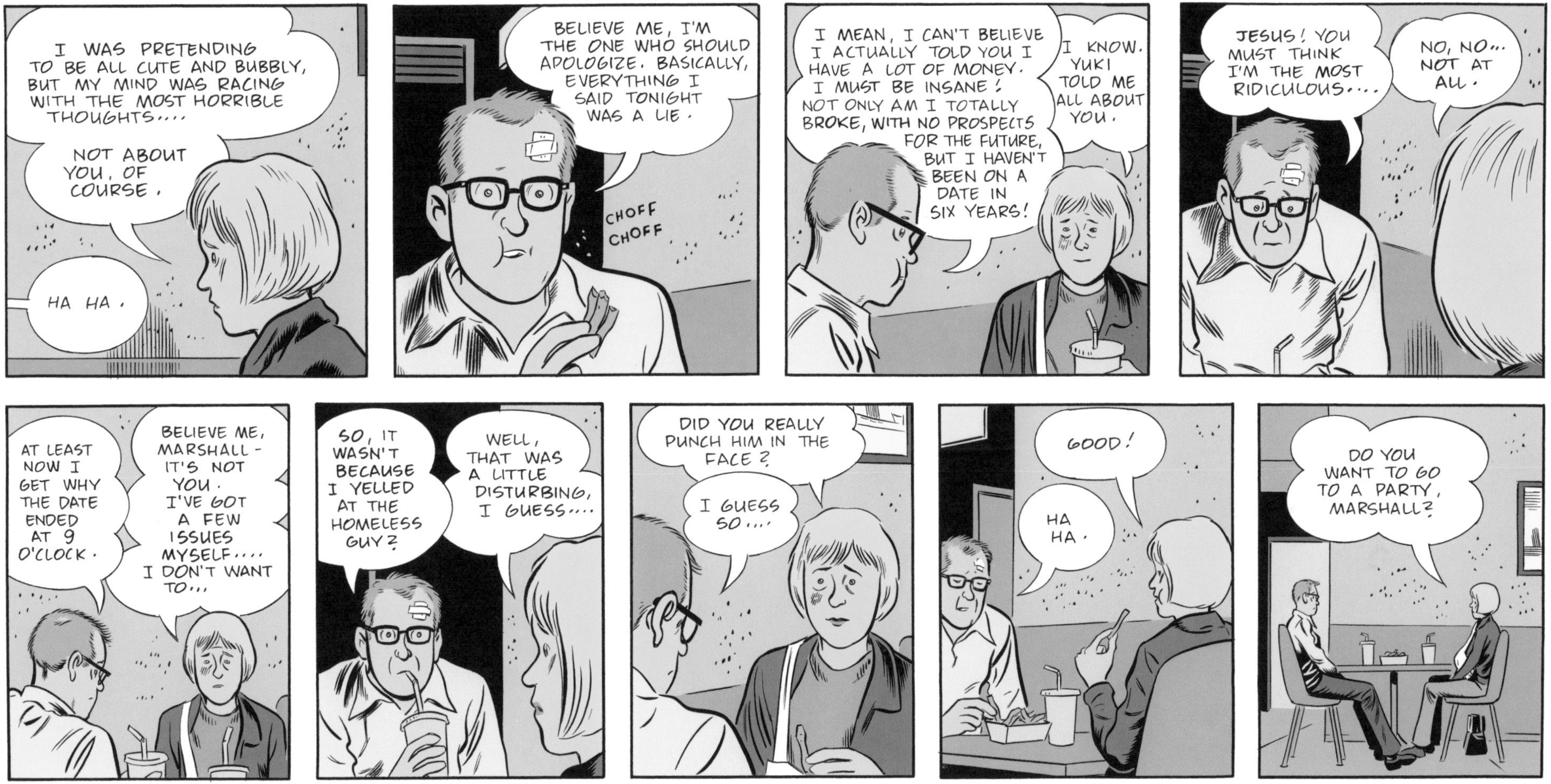
I WAS PRETENDING TO BE ALL CUTE AND BUBBLY, BUT MY MIND WAS RACING WITH THE MOST HORRIBLE THOUGHTS....
NOT ABOUT YOU, OF COURSE.
HA HA.
BELIEVE ME, I'M THE ONE WHO SHOULD APOLOGIZE. BASICALLY, EVERYTHING I SAID TONIGHT WAS A LIE.
CHOFF CHOFF
I MEAN, I CAN'T BELIEVE I ACTUALLY TOLD YOU I HAVE A LOT OF MONEY. I MUST BE INSANE! NOT ONLY AM I TOTALLY BROKE, WITH NO PROSPECTS FOR THE FUTURE, BUT I HAVEN'T BEEN ON A DATE IN SIX YEARS!
I KNOW. YUKI TOLD ME ALL ABOUT YOU.
JESUS! YOU MUST THINK I'M THE MOST RIDICULOUS....
NO, NO... NOT AT ALL.
AT LEAST NOW I GET WHY THE DATE ENDED AT 9 O'CLOCK.
BELIEVE ME, MARSHALL - IT'S NOT YOU. I'VE GOT A FEW ISSUES MYSELF.... I DON'T WANT TO...
SO, IT WASN'T BECAUSE I YELLED AT THE HOMELESS GUY?
WELL, THAT WAS A LITTLE DISTURBING, I GUESS....
DID YOU REALLY PUNCH HIM IN THE FACE?
I GUESS SO....
GOOD!
HA HA.
DO YOU WANT TO GO TO A PARTY, MARSHALL?

BRRRRMRR

RBLLBRRRRR

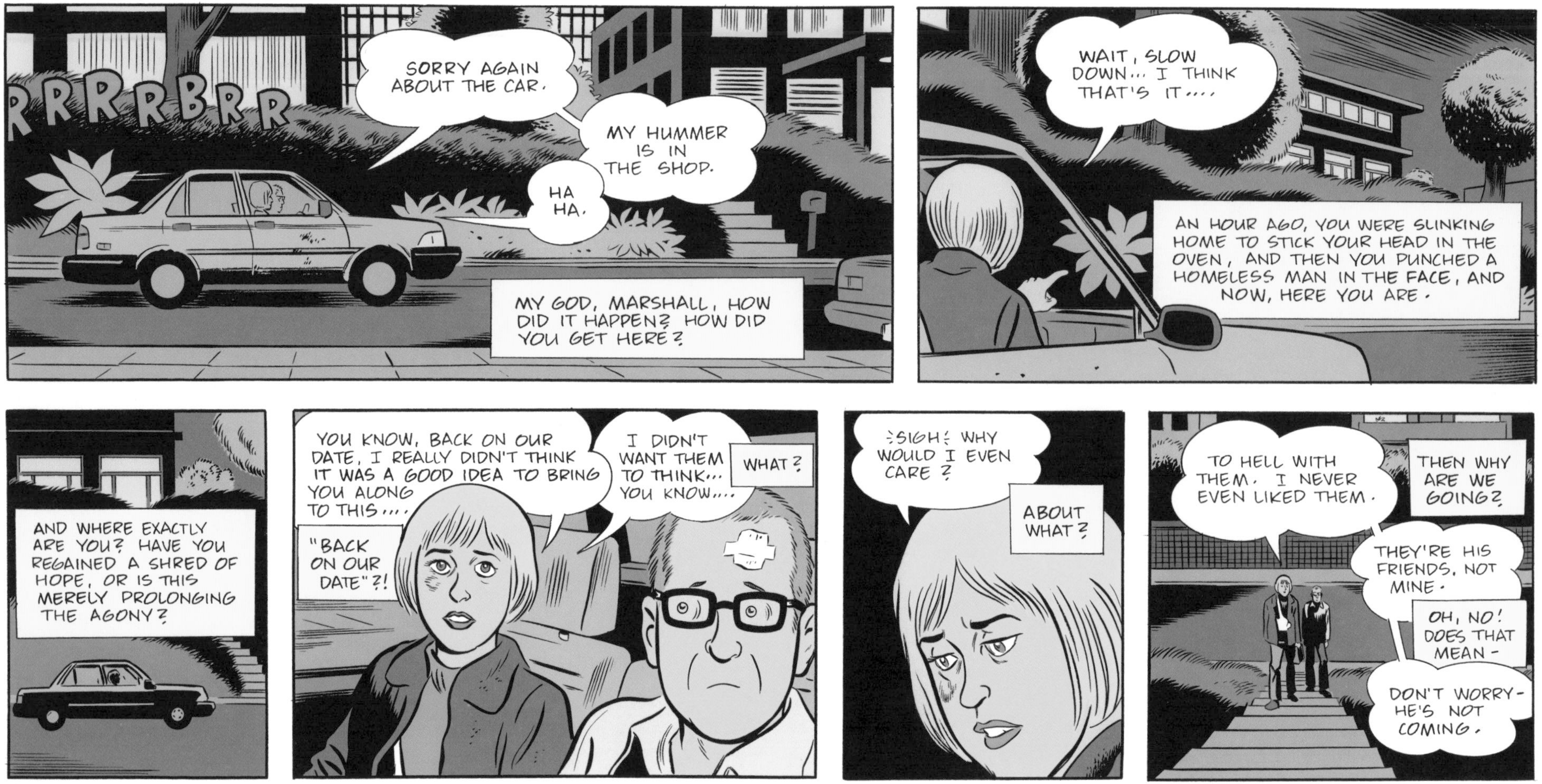
RRRRBRRR
SORRY AGAIN ABOUT THE CAR.
MY HUMMER IS IN THE SHOP.
HA HA.
MY GOD, MARSHALL, HOW DID IT HAPPEN? HOW DID YOU GET HERE?
WAIT, SLOW DOWN... I THINK THAT'S IT....
AN HOUR AGO, YOU WERE SLINKING HOME TO STICK YOUR HEAD IN THE OVEN, AND THEN YOU PUNCHED A HOMELESS MAN IN THE FACE, AND NOW, HERE YOU ARE.
AND WHERE EXACTLY ARE YOU? HAVE YOU REGAINED A SHRED OF HOPE, OR IS THIS MERELY PROLONGING THE AGONY?
YOU KNOW, BACK ON OUR DATE, I REALLY DIDN'T THINK IT WAS A GOOD IDEA TO BRING YOU ALONG TO THIS....
"BACK ON OUR DATE"?!
I DIDN'T WANT THEM TO THINK... YOU KNOW....
WHAT?
÷SIGH÷ WHY WOULD I EVEN CARE?
ABOUT WHAT?
TO HELL WITH THEM. I NEVER EVEN LIKED THEM.
THEN WHY ARE WE GOING?
THEY'RE HIS FRIENDS, NOT MINE.
OH, NO! DOES THAT MEAN -
DON'T WORRY- HE'S NOT COMING.

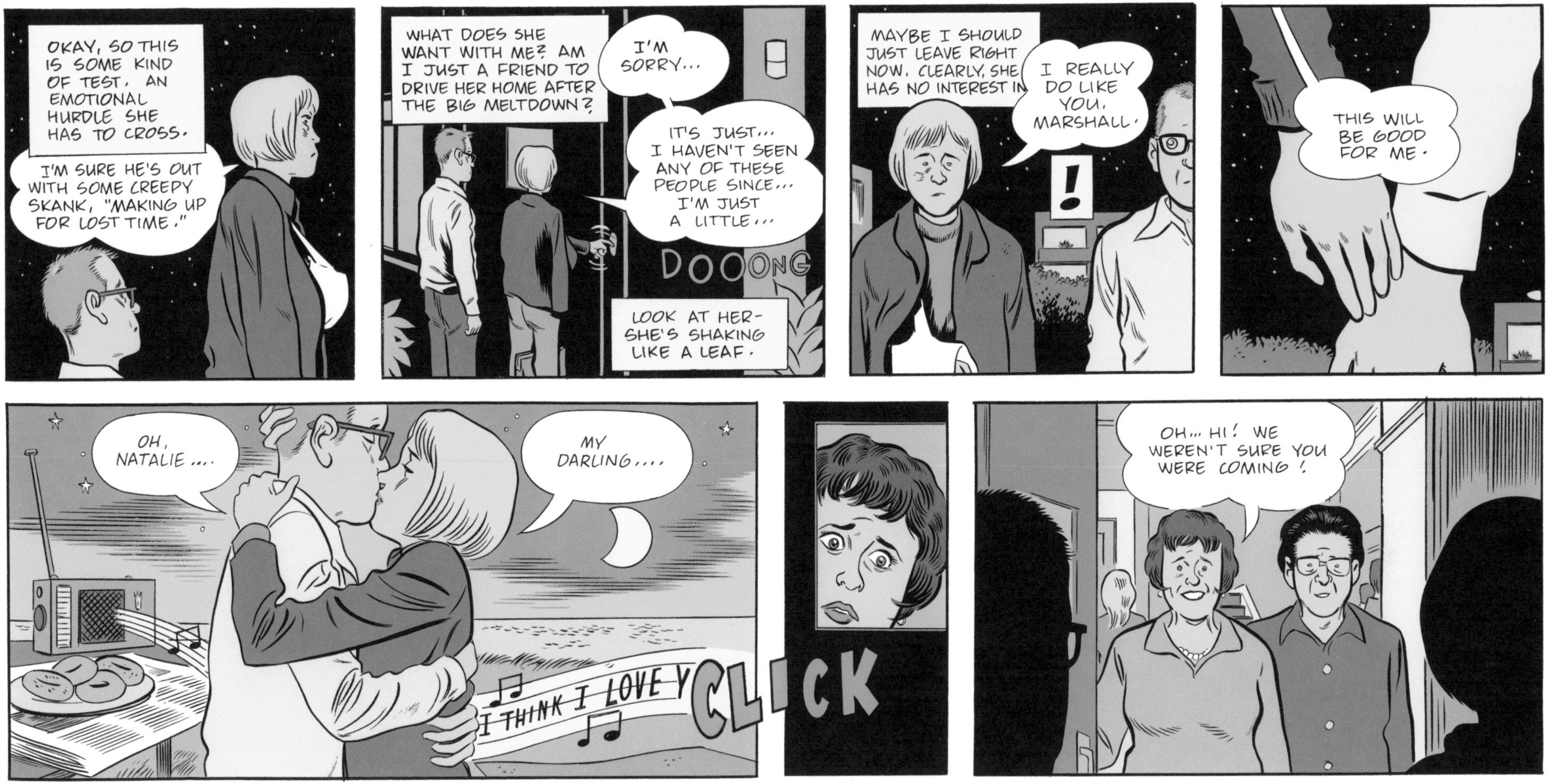

OKAY, SO THIS IS SOME KIND OF TEST. AN EMOTIONAL HURDLE SHE HAS TO CROSS.
I'M SURE HE'S OUT WITH SOME CREEPY SKANK, "MAKING UP FOR LOST TIME."
WHAT DOES SHE WANT WITH ME? AM I JUST A FRIEND TO DRIVE HER HOME AFTER THE BIG MELTDOWN?
I'M SORRY...
IT'S JUST... I HAVEN'T SEEN ANY OF THESE PEOPLE SINCE... I'M JUST A LITTLE...
DOOOONG
LOOK AT HER- SHE'S SHAKING LIKE A LEAF.
MAYBE I SHOULD JUST LEAVE RIGHT NOW. CLEARLY, SHE HAS NO INTEREST IN
I REALLY DO LIKE YOU, MARSHALL.
!
THIS WILL BE GOOD FOR ME.
OH, NATALIE....
MY DARLING....
I THINK I LOVE Y
CLICK
OH... HI! WE WEREN'T SURE YOU WERE COMING!

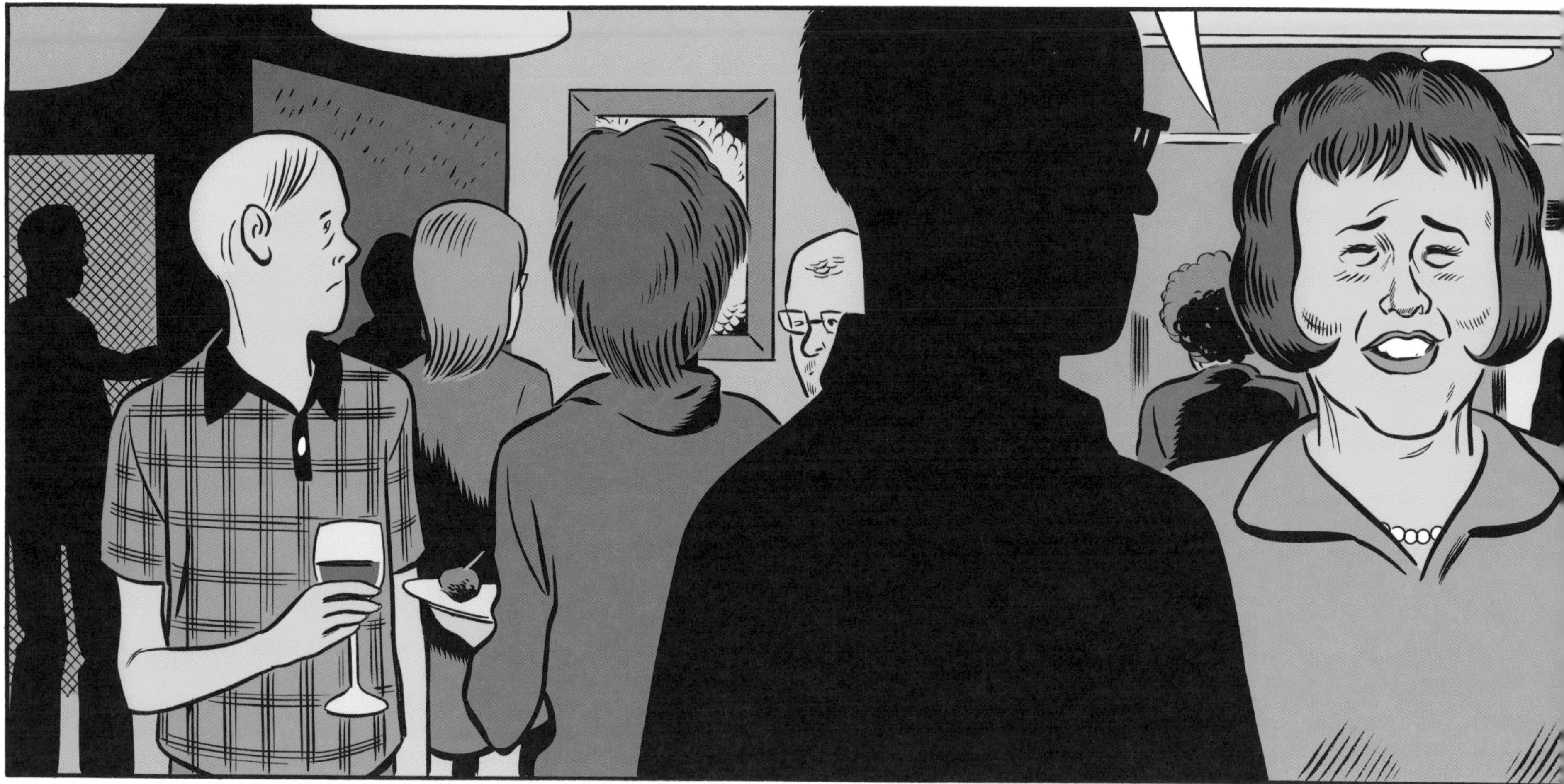

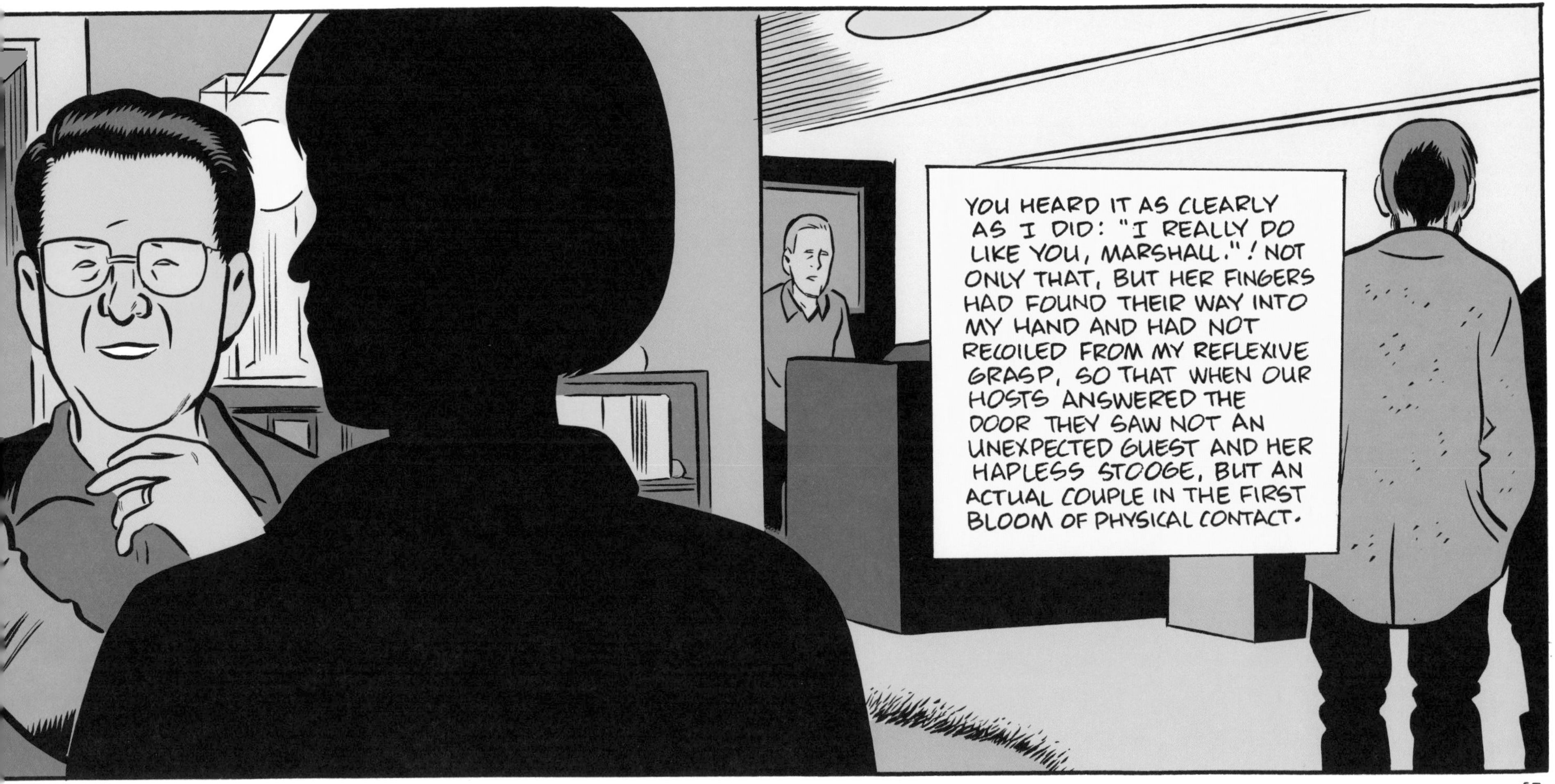
YOU HEARD IT AS CLEARLY AS I DID: "I REALLY DO LIKE YOU, MARSHALL."! NOT ONLY THAT, BUT HER FINGERS HAD FOUND THEIR WAY INTO MY HAND AND HAD NOT RECOILED FROM MY REFLEXIVE GRASP, SO THAT WHEN OUR HOSTS ANSWERED THE DOOR THEY SAW NOT AN UNEXPECTED GUEST AND HER HAPLESS STOOGE, BUT AN ACTUAL COUPLE IN THE FIRST BLOOM OF PHYSICAL CONTACT.

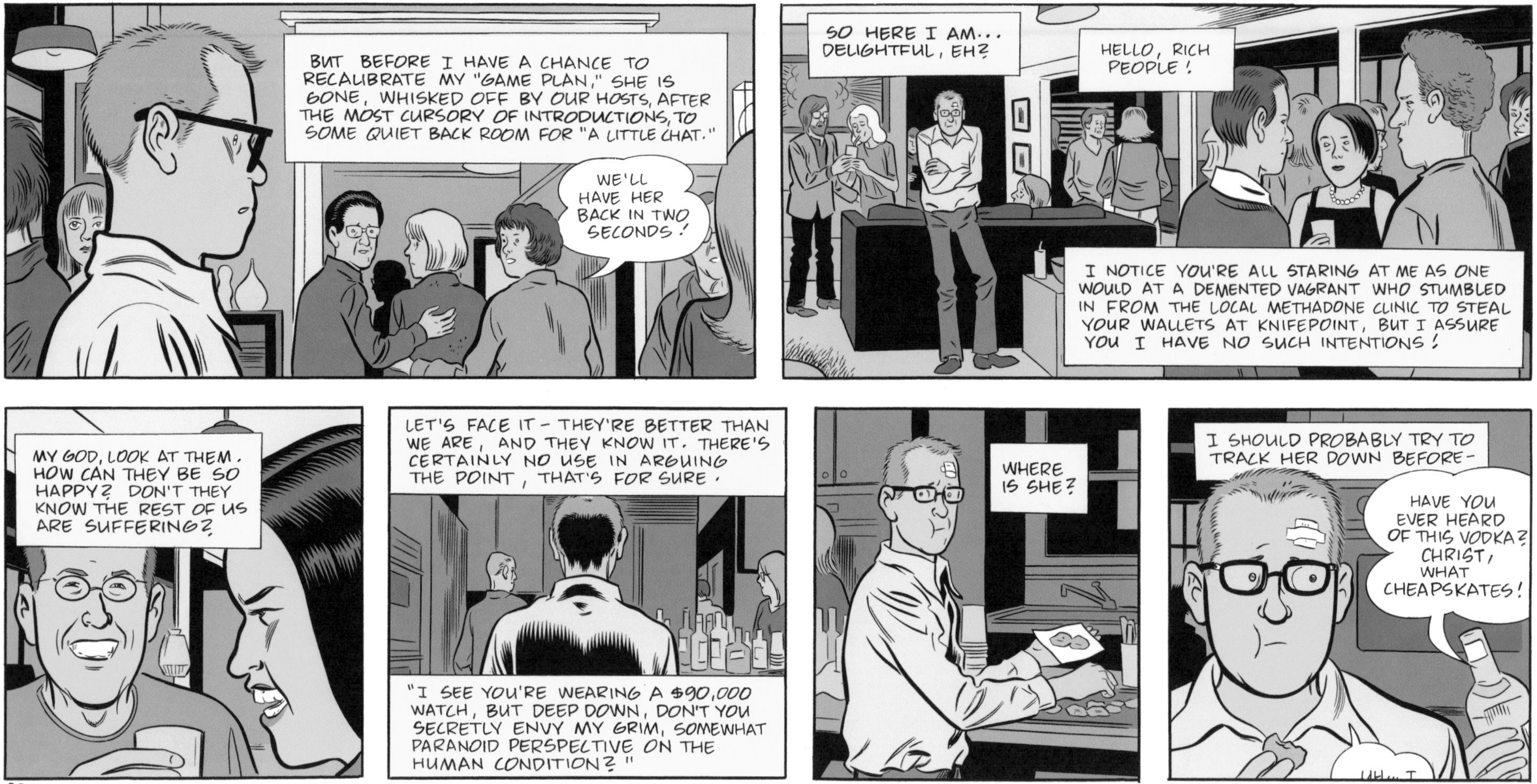

BUT BEFORE I HAVE A CHANCE TO RECALIBRATE MY "GAME PLAN," SHE IS GONE, WHISKED OFF BY OUR HOSTS, AFTER THE MOST CURSORY OF INTRODUCTIONS, TO SOME QUIET BACK ROOM FOR "A LITTLE CHAT."
WE'LL HAVE HER BACK IN TWO SECONDS!
SO HERE I AM... DELIGHTFUL, EH?
HELLO, RICH PEOPLE!
I NOTICE YOU'RE ALL STARING AT ME AS ONE WOULD AT A DEMENTED VAGRANT WHO STUMBLED IN FROM THE LOCAL METHADONE CLINIC TO STEAL YOUR WALLETS AT KNIFEPOINT, BUT I ASSURE YOU I HAVE NO SUCH INTENTIONS!
MY GOD, LOOK AT THEM. HOW CAN THEY BE SO HAPPY? DON'T THEY KNOW THE REST OF US ARE SUFFERING?
LET'S FACE IT - THEY'RE BETTER THAN WE ARE, AND THEY KNOW IT. THERE'S CERTAINLY NO USE IN ARGUING THE POINT, THAT'S FOR SURE.
"I SEE YOU'RE WEARING A $90,000 WATCH, BUT DEEP DOWN, DON'T YOU SECRETLY ENVY MY GRIM, SOMEWHAT PARANOID PERSPECTIVE ON THE HUMAN CONDITION?"
WHERE IS SHE?
I SHOULD PROBABLY TRY TO TRACK HER DOWN BEFORE-
HAVE YOU EVER HEARD OF THIS VODKA? CHRIST, WHAT CHEAPSKATES!

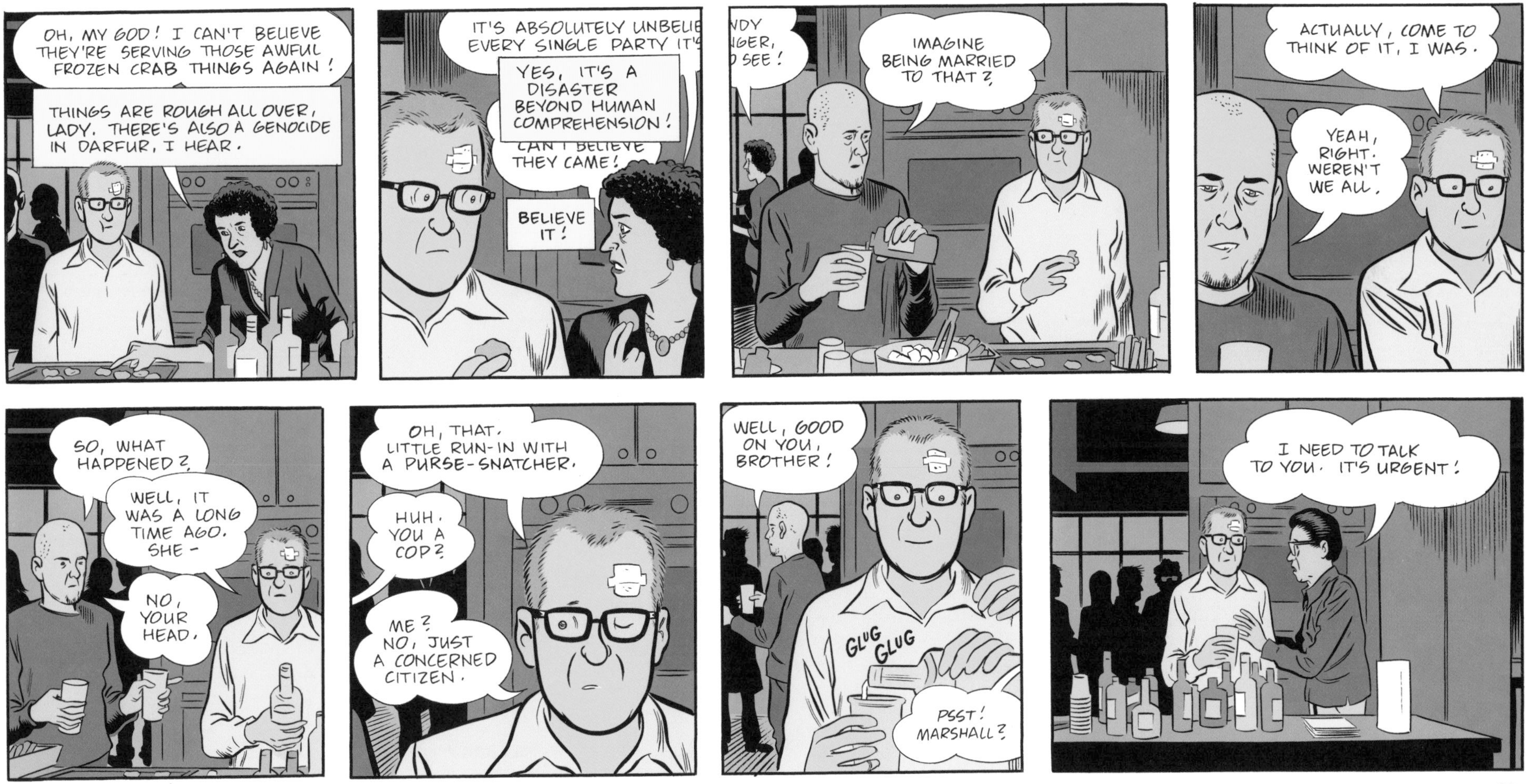

OH, MY GOD! I CAN'T BELIEVE THEY'RE SERVING THOSE AWFUL FROZEN CRAB THINGS AGAIN!
THINGS ARE ROUGH ALL OVER, LADY. THERE'S ALSO A GENOCIDE IN DARFUR, I HEAR.
IT'S ABSOLUTELY UNBELIE
EVERY SINGLE PARTY IT'S
YES, IT'S A DISASTER BEYOND HUMAN COMPREHENSION!
THEY CAME!
BELIEVE IT!
IMAGINE BEING MARRIED TO THAT?
ACTUALLY, COME TO THINK OF IT, I WAS.
YEAH, RIGHT. WEREN'T WE ALL.
SO, WHAT HAPPENED?
WELL, IT WAS A LONG TIME AGO. SHE -
NO, YOUR HEAD.
OH, THAT. LITTLE RUN-IN WITH A PURSE-SNATCHER.
HUH. YOU A COP?
ME? NO, JUST A CONCERNED CITIZEN.
WELL, GOOD ON YOU, BROTHER!
GLUG GLUG
PSST! MARSHALL?
I NEED TO TALK TO YOU. IT'S URGENT!

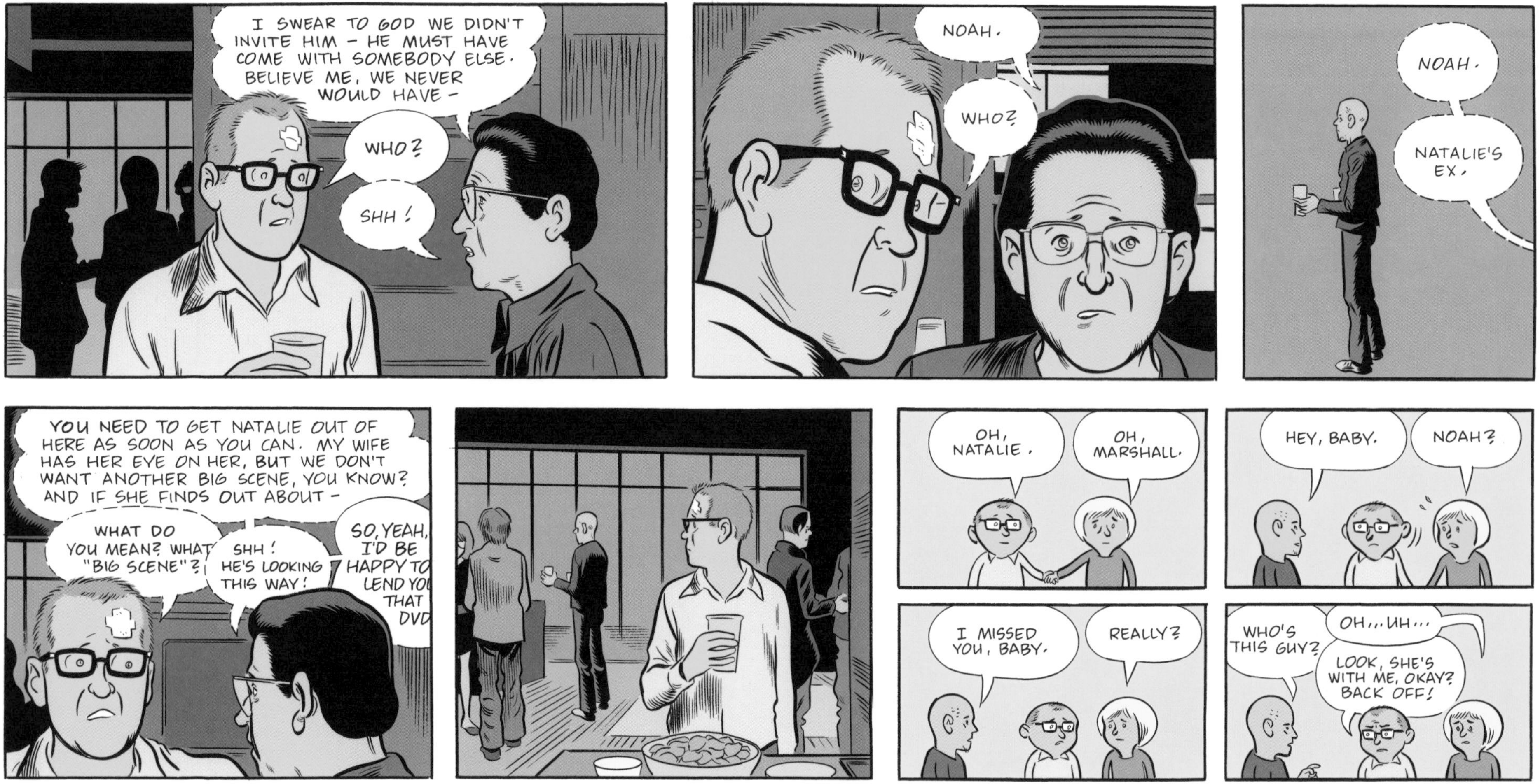
I SWEAR TO GOD WE DIDN'T INVITE HIM - HE MUST HAVE COME WITH SOMEBODY ELSE. BELIEVE ME, WE NEVER WOULD HAVE -
WHO?
SHH!
NOAH.
WHO?
NOAH.
NATALIE'S EX.
YOU NEED TO GET NATALIE OUT OF HERE AS SOON AS YOU CAN. MY WIFE HAS HER EYE ON HER, BUT WE DON'T WANT ANOTHER BIG SCENE, YOU KNOW? AND IF SHE FINDS OUT ABOUT -
WHAT DO YOU MEAN? WHAT "BIG SCENE"?
SHH! HE'S LOOKING THIS WAY!
SO, YEAH, I'D BE HAPPY TO LEND YOU THAT DVD
OH, NATALIE.
OH, MARSHALL.
HEY, BABY.
NOAH?
I MISSED YOU, BABY.
REALLY?
WHO'S THIS GUY?
OH... UH...
LOOK, SHE'S WITH ME, OKAY? BACK OFF!

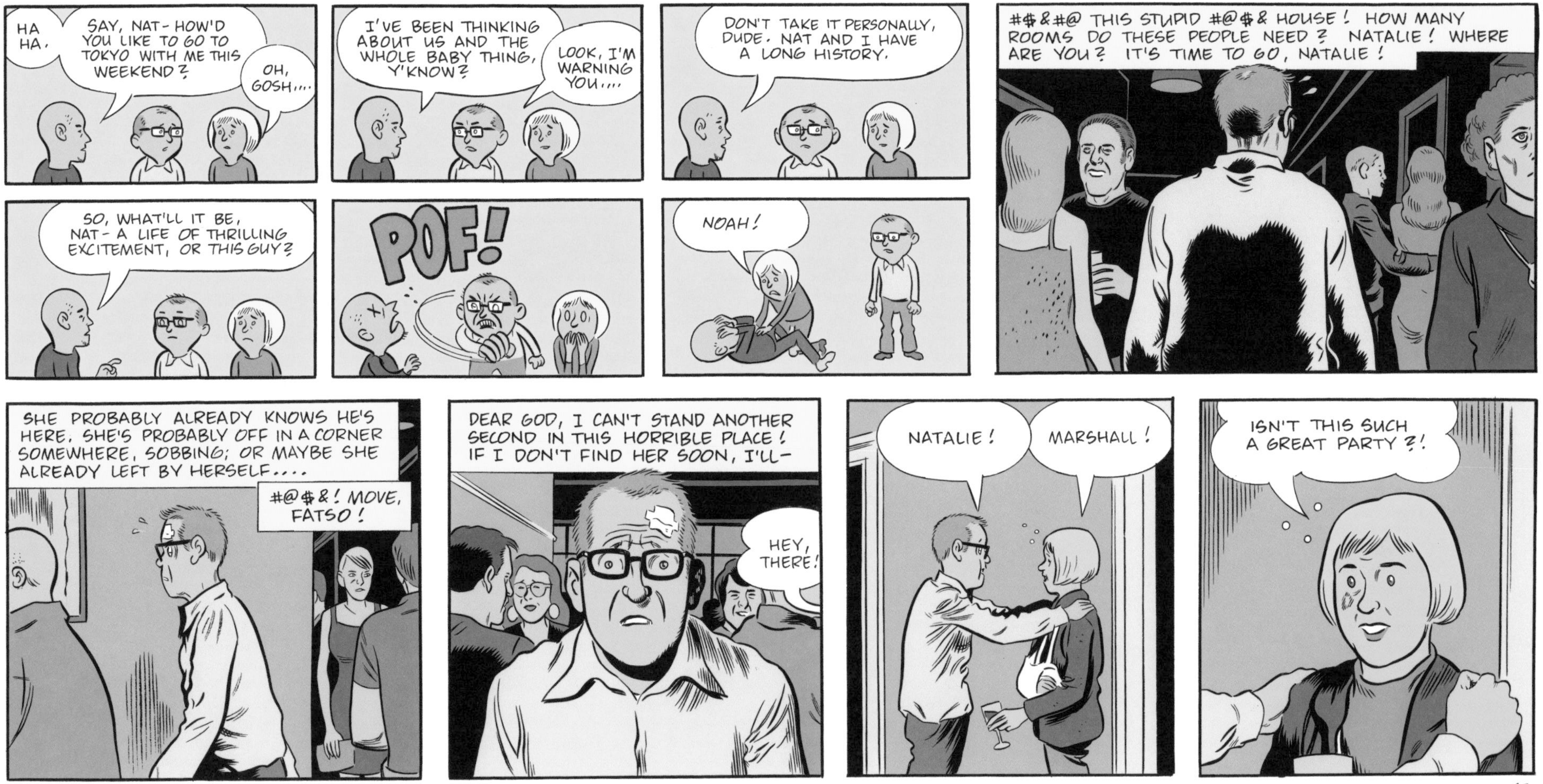
HA HA.
SAY, NAT- HOW'D YOU LIKE TO GO TO TOKYO WITH ME THIS WEEKEND?
OH, GOSH....
I'VE BEEN THINKING ABOUT US AND THE WHOLE BABY THING, Y'KNOW?
LOOK, I'M WARNING YOU....
DON'T TAKE IT PERSONALLY, DUDE. NAT AND I HAVE A LONG HISTORY.
#$&#@ THIS STUPID #@$& HOUSE! HOW MANY ROOMS DO THESE PEOPLE NEED? NATALIE! WHERE ARE YOU? IT'S TIME TO GO, NATALIE!
SO, WHAT'LL IT BE, NAT- A LIFE OF THRILLING EXCITEMENT, OR THIS GUY?
POF!
NOAH!
SHE PROBABLY ALREADY KNOWS HE'S HERE. SHE'S PROBABLY OFF IN A CORNER SOMEWHERE, SOBBING; OR MAYBE SHE ALREADY LEFT BY HERSELF....
#@$&! MOVE, FATSO!
DEAR GOD, I CAN'T STAND ANOTHER SECOND IN THIS HORRIBLE PLACE! IF I DON'T FIND HER SOON, I'LL-
HEY, THERE!
NATALIE!
MARSHALL!
ISN'T THIS SUCH A GREAT PARTY?!

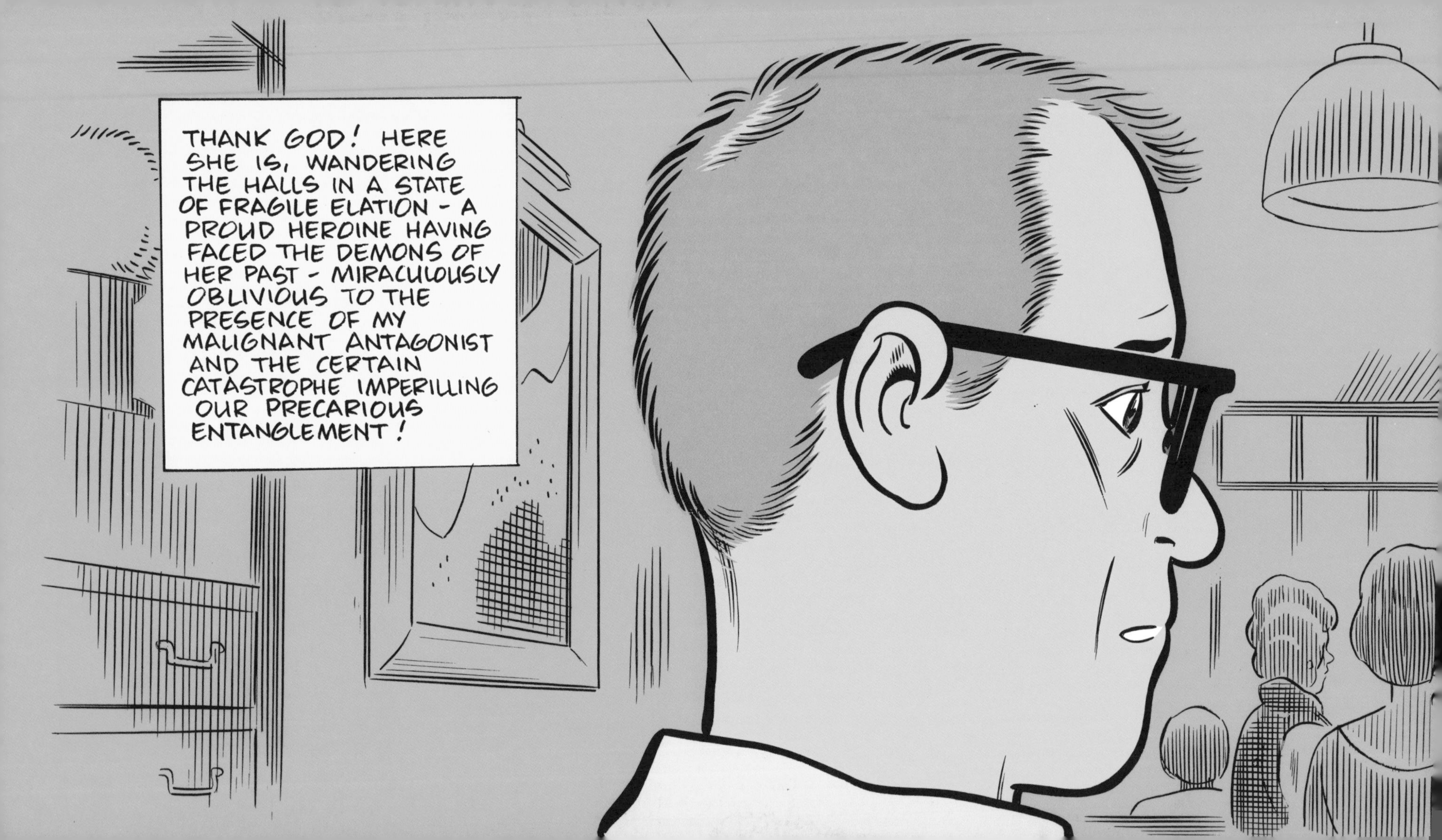
THANK GOD! HERE SHE IS, WANDERING THE HALLS IN A STATE OF FRAGILE ELATION - A PROUD HEROINE HAVING FACED THE DEMONS OF HER PAST - MIRACULOUSLY OBLIVIOUS TO THE PRESENCE OF MY MALIGNANT ANTAGONIST AND THE CERTAIN CATASTROPHE IMPERILLING OUR PRECARIOUS ENTANGLEMENT!

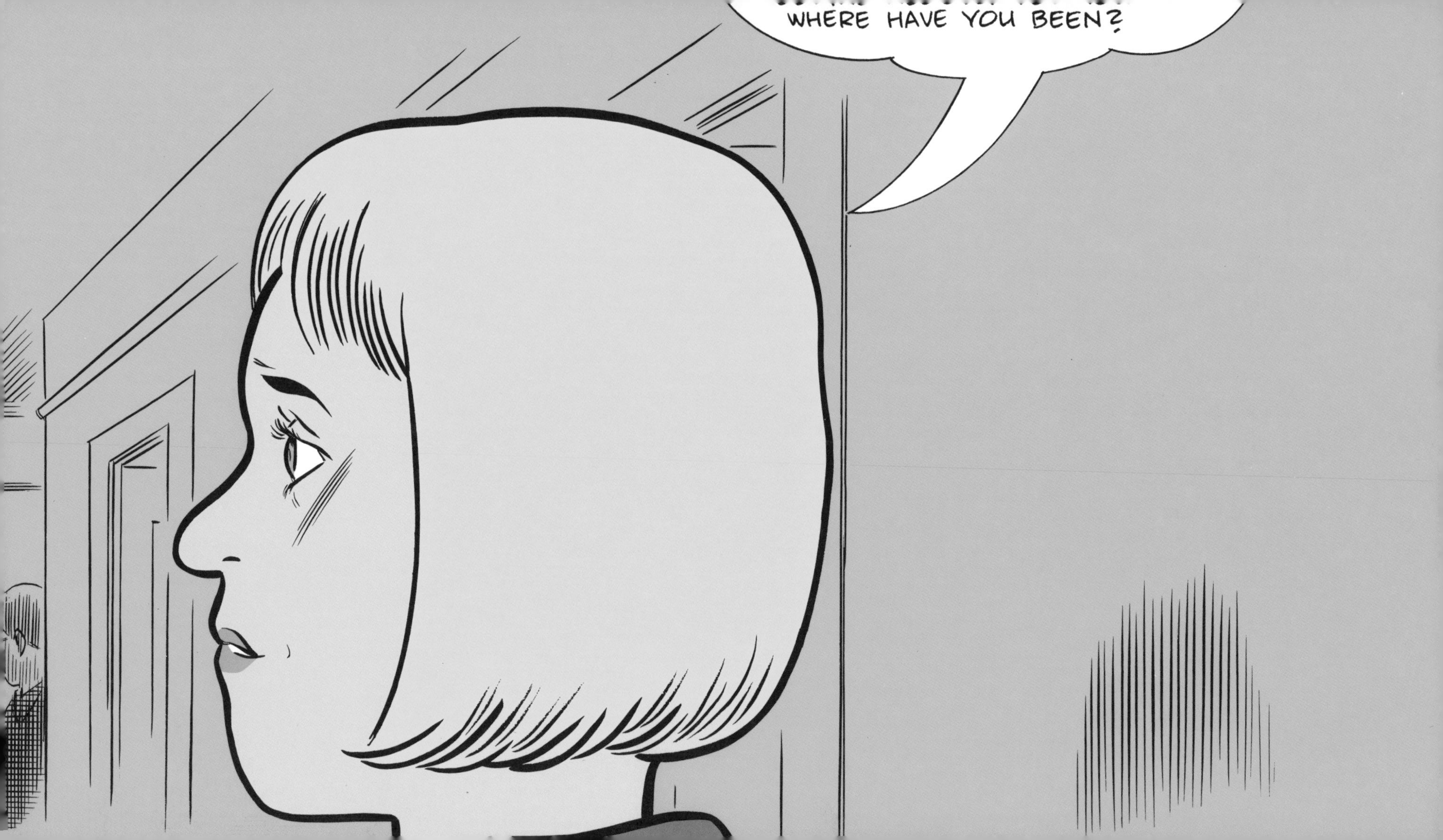
WHERE HAVE YOU BEEN?

I'M REALLY SORRY I ABANDONED YOU - GOD, YOU MUST BE SO BORED! IS THER... ...RTH TALKING TO? D... ...'T GO AWAY ANY MO... ...IEVED IT ISN'T A...

OKAY, THINK MARSHALL. WHAT'S YOUR PLAN?

GOD, I'M TOTALLY DRUNK! I... ARE YOU OKAY?

GREAT, GREAT...

SO, I GUESS MAYBE I'M GETTING A LITTLE TIRED....

POP!

HOLD ON, CHIEF— THAT "HONESTY" GIMMICK WAS WORKING PRETTY GOOD BACK IN THE HOSPITAL...

MAYBE YOU OUGHTA JUST TELL HER ABOUT THE EX.

SHE'S A BIG GIRL— SHE'LL PROBABLY THINK IT'S FUNNY! AND YOU'RE GONNA HAVE TO TELL HER AT SO^ AKKKK

CRUS...

YEAH, I MEAN, I'M MORE THAN HAPPY TO STAY, BUT I JUST THIN...

I'M NOT ONE FOR THE HARD SELL, BUT DESPERATE TIMES CALL FOR ETC., ETC., AND SO, IN A MOMENT OF PANIC-INDUCED LUCIDITY, I SOMEHOW FIND THE WORDS TO MOUNT A PERSUASIVE PITCH.

...ON A HIGH NOTE.

MAYBE YOU'RE RIGHT.

I GUESS IT'S A MATTER OF T... BEFORE SOME... SAYS SOMETHI...

INCREDIBLE! IT LOOKS AS IF WE MAY ACTUALLY—

NATALIE? IS THAT YOU?

#@&$!

OH, NO – THIS ONE AGAIN! IF YOU SO MUCH AS MENTION NOAH'S NAME, I'LL MURDER YOU RIGHT HERE ON THE SPOT, YOU MISERABLE....

...HAT...ED...RM?

YES, HA HA....

OH, IT'S... JUST A...

OH, MY GOD – I HAVEN'T TOLD YOU ABOUT OUR NEW HOUSE!

BLAH, BLAH, BLAH! WRAP IT UP, LADY! THE METER'S RUNNING!

LUCKILY, HER LITTLE MONOLOGUE IS SO SELF-CENTERED, SHE DOESN'T HAVE ROOM FOR–

JUST BE THANKFUL YOU DON'T HAVE KIDS! I NEVER... OUCH! ...MINUTE TO MYSELF!

THAT CERTAINLY WASN'T THE MOST SENSITIVE THING TO SAY TO A CHILDLESS 39-YEAR-OLD.

YEAH, WELL, WE WERE JUST LEAVING.

THANK YOU, HORRIBLE WOMAN! NOW IF WE CAN JUST MAKE IT TO THE DOOR....

YOU'RE RIGHT – IT'S TIME TO GO.

DEAR GOD, IS IT POSSIBLE? ARE WE ACTUALLY GOING TO–

OOPS, I FORGOT MY PURSE!

#@$&!

I'LL BE–

NO! YOU WAIT RIGHT HERE – I'LL GET IT!

OKAY, MARSHALL– STAY CALM! THIS IS NO TIME TO LOSE...

WHERE'S THE @$* COAT ROOM?

HAVE YOU SEEN A RED PURSE?

IT SHOULD BE RIGHT H–

IT'S... UH...

65.

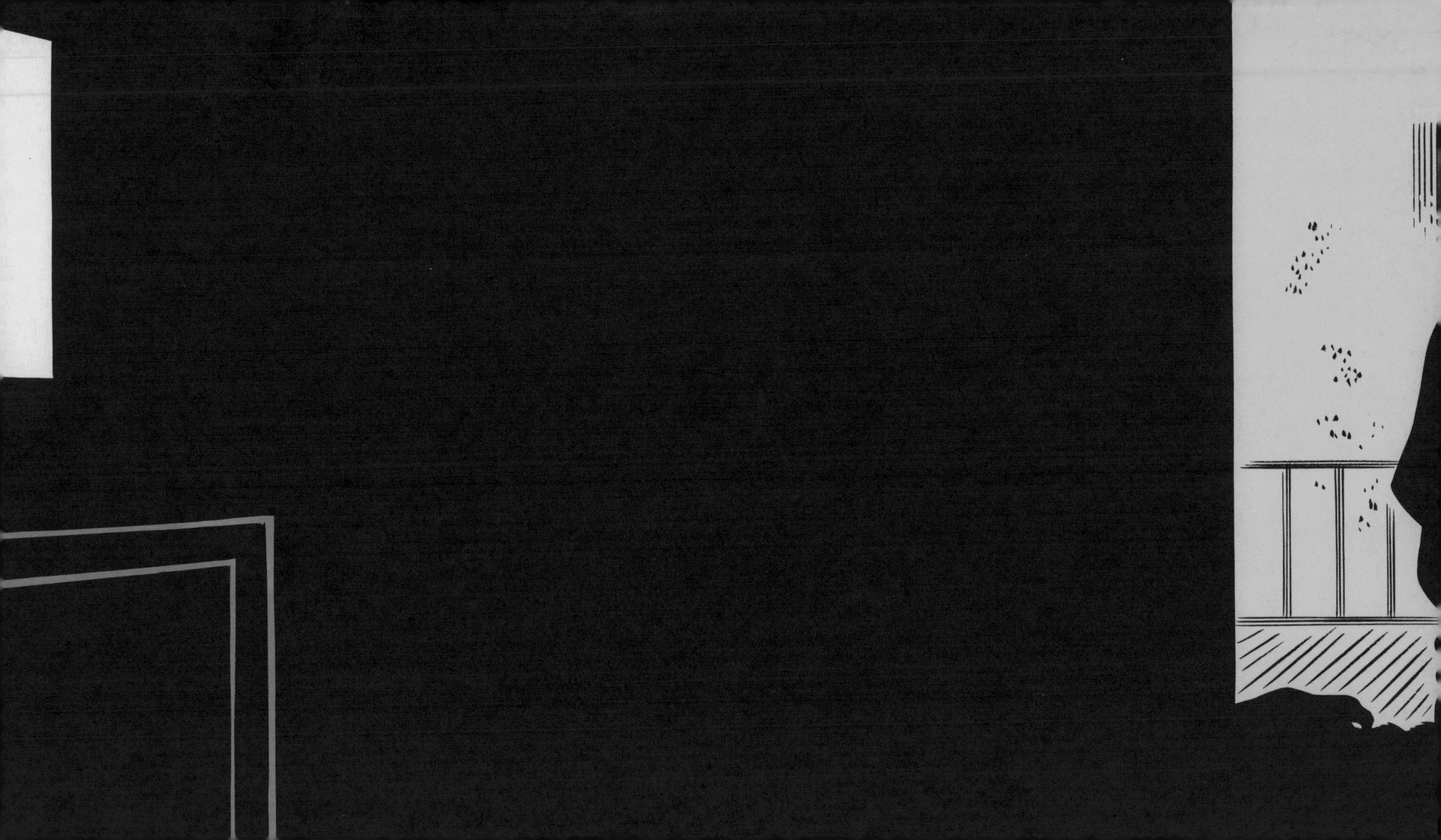

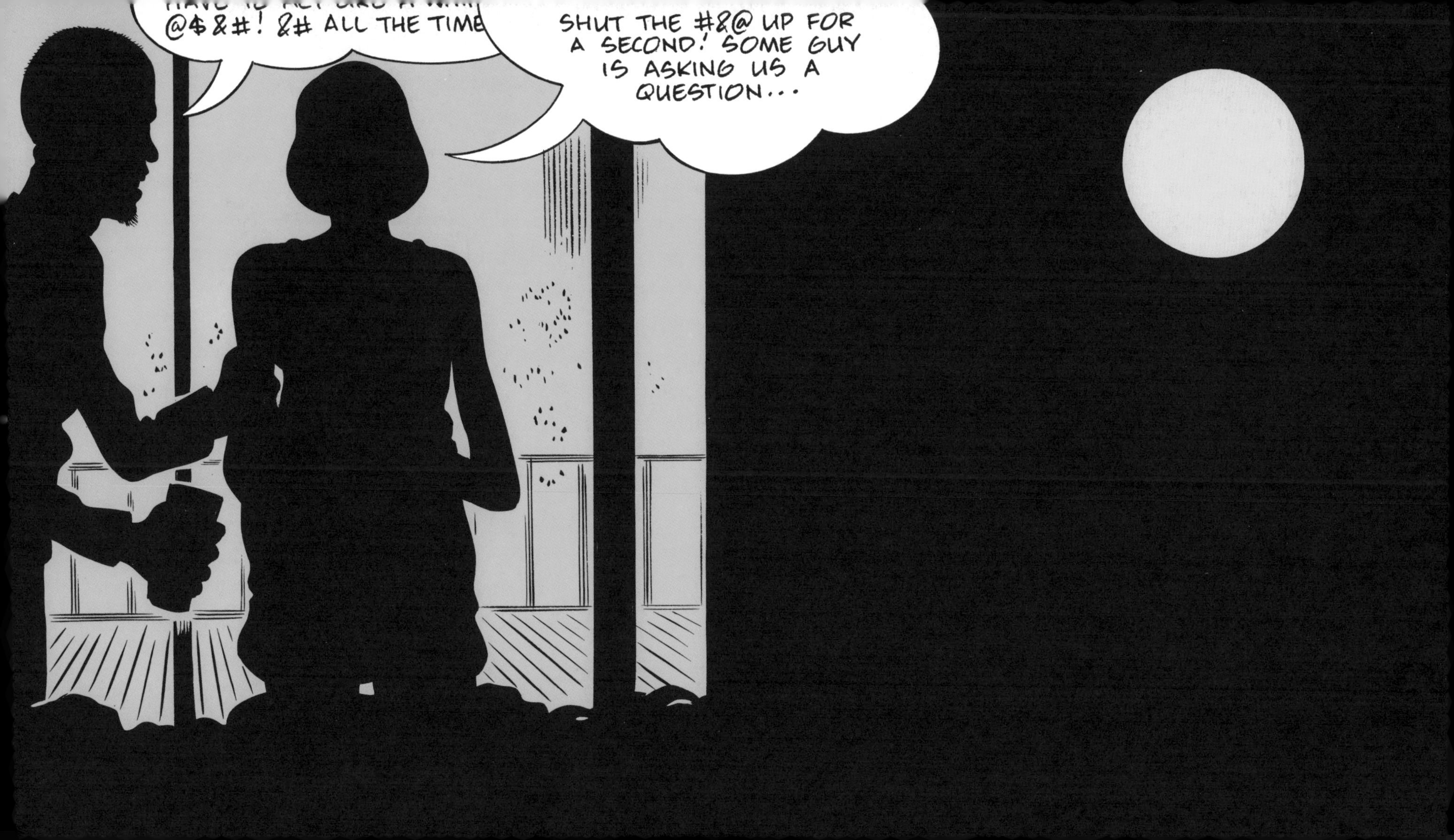
@$&#! &# ALL THE TIME
SHUT THE #&@ UP FOR A SECOND! SOME GUY IS ASKING US A QUESTION...

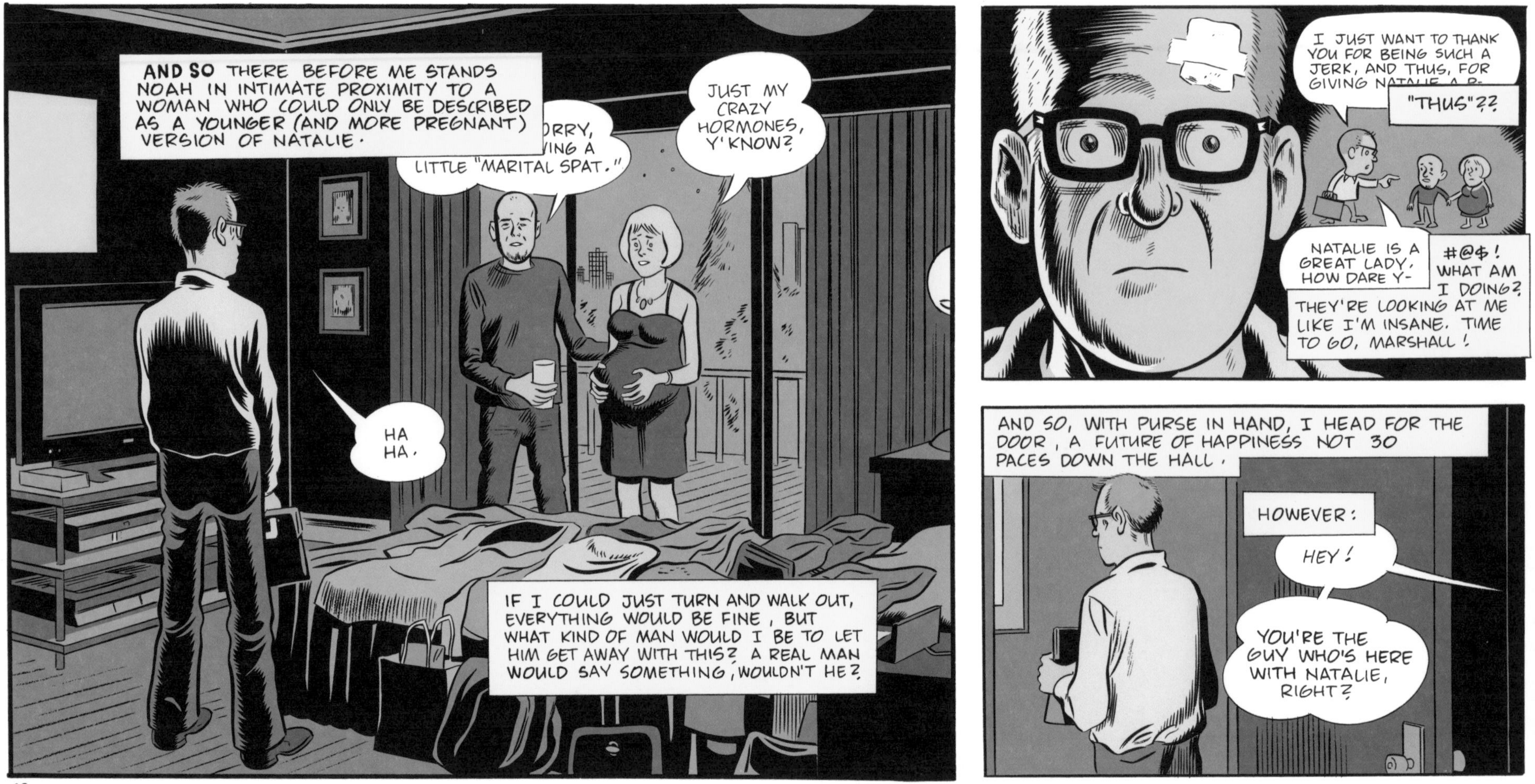
AND SO THERE BEFORE ME STANDS NOAH IN INTIMATE PROXIMITY TO A WOMAN WHO COULD ONLY BE DESCRIBED AS A YOUNGER (AND MORE PREGNANT) VERSION OF NATALIE.
ORRY, VING A LITTLE "MARITAL SPAT."
JUST MY CRAZY HORMONES, Y'KNOW?
HA HA.
IF I COULD JUST TURN AND WALK OUT, EVERYTHING WOULD BE FINE, BUT WHAT KIND OF MAN WOULD I BE TO LET HIM GET AWAY WITH THIS? A REAL MAN WOULD SAY SOMETHING, WOULDN'T HE?
I JUST WANT TO THANK YOU FOR BEING SUCH A JERK, AND THUS, FOR GIVING NAT
"THUS"??
NATALIE IS A GREAT LADY, HOW DARE Y-
#@$! WHAT AM I DOING?
THEY'RE LOOKING AT ME LIKE I'M INSANE. TIME TO GO, MARSHALL!
AND SO, WITH PURSE IN HAND, I HEAD FOR THE DOOR, A FUTURE OF HAPPINESS NOT 30 PACES DOWN THE HALL.
HOWEVER:
HEY!
YOU'RE THE GUY WHO'S HERE WITH NATALIE, RIGHT?

I AM.

WORD OF WARNING, BROTHER— YOU'RE IN FOR A WORLD OF TROUBLE!

TEE HEE

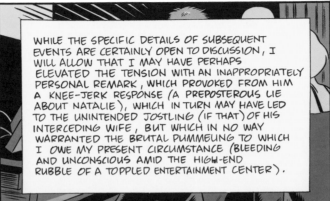

WHILE THE SPECIFIC DETAILS OF SUBSEQUENT EVENTS ARE CERTAINLY OPEN TO DISCUSSION, I WILL ALLOW THAT I MAY HAVE PERHAPS ELEVATED THE TENSION WITH AN INAPPROPRIATELY PERSONAL REMARK, WHICH PROVOKED FROM HIM A KNEE-JERK RESPONSE (A PREPOSTEROUS LIE ABOUT NATALIE), WHICH IN TURN MAY HAVE LED TO THE UNINTENDED JOSTLING (IF THAT) OF HIS INTERCEDING WIFE, BUT WHICH IN NO WAY WARRANTED THE BRUTAL PUMMELING TO WHICH I OWE MY PRESENT CIRCUMSTANCE (BLEEDING AND UNCONSCIOUS AMID THE HIGH-END RUBBLE OF A TOPPLED ENTERTAINMENT CENTER).

YOU NEED TO GET OUT OF HERE RIGHT NOW!

C'MON, GET UP!

NATALIE?

FORGET ABOUT HER! THAT'S NOT GONNA WORK OUT, OKAY? NOW GET UP AND GET OUT BEFORE I CALL THE COPS!

THERE SHE IS. NOT EVEN A GLANCE AT HER FALLEN HERO.

LOOK, I DON'T EVEN KNOW YOU— YOU'RE PROBABLY A GOOD GUY, BUT SHE'S JUST NOT IN A PLACE WHERE SHE

IT'S OKAY, FRIEND— YOU CAN STOP NOW.

BELIEVE ME, I GET THE PICTURE.

I'M GLAD THE STUPID TV GOT BROKEN. WHO THE #@$# CARES?

IN A WORLD LIKE THIS, TO EVEN THINK ABOUT CONSUMER ELECTRONICS... IT'S UNFORGIVABLE.

IF THOSE ARE HER FRIENDS, WHO NEEDS HER? "YOUR NINTH BIG-SCREEN TV GOT BROKEN - WELL, BOO-HOO!"..."I'VE GOT A SOLUTION: BUY ANOTHER ONE!"

GUYS KNOW A GUY NAMED RANDY?

SPARE A DOLLAR?

YOU G A DOLL

DOLLA

IT'S KIND OF A RELIEF, TO BE HONEST. I DON'T KNOW IF I COULD HANDLE THE PRESSURE OF A RELATIONSHIP WITH SOMEONE LIKE THAT.

WHAT WOULD IT SOLVE, ANYWAY? NOTHING, REALLY.... I NEED TO ACCEPT THE TRUTH AND MOVE ON.

HELL, I UP NEEDING FROM YOU, SOMEDAY.

VER TV!

IF THOSE ARE HE FRIENDS, WHO NE HER, RIGHT?

THE IMPORTANT THING IS TO MAKE A CLEAN BREAK.

I'M NOT GOING TO BEG SOMEONE TO LOVE ME! I'M A GOOD PERSON!

YOU GE WHAT I MEAN RIGHT

IF I HAD A BLADE, I'D SLICE YOUR THROAT AND LEAVE YOU FOR DEAD!

I ENTER THIS APARTMENT A DIFFERENT MAN FROM THE ONE WHO LEFT IT. THIS IS THE BEGINNING OF A WHOLE NEW MARSHALL....

OH, GOD... I FORGOT I CLEANED THE PLACE UP.

EVEN IF BY SOME MIRACLE I WAS ABLE TO LURE HER BACK TO MY DANK HOVEL, DID I REALLY IMAGINE I WOULD "GET LUCKY" WHEN SHE SAW HOW NEATLY I STACKED MY DISTURBING HEAPS OF PACK-RAT JUNK?

YOU HAVE NO NEW MESSAGES.

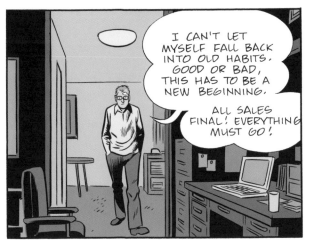

I CAN'T LET MYSELF FALL BACK INTO OLD HABITS. GOOD OR BAD, THIS HAS TO BE A NEW BEGINNING.

ALL SALES FINAL! EVERYTHING MUST GO!

#@$#&@#!! OUTBID AGAIN. #@*$ LUCKYMOJO55!

CLICK CLICK

WAIT A MINUTE... WHAT THE #@$*

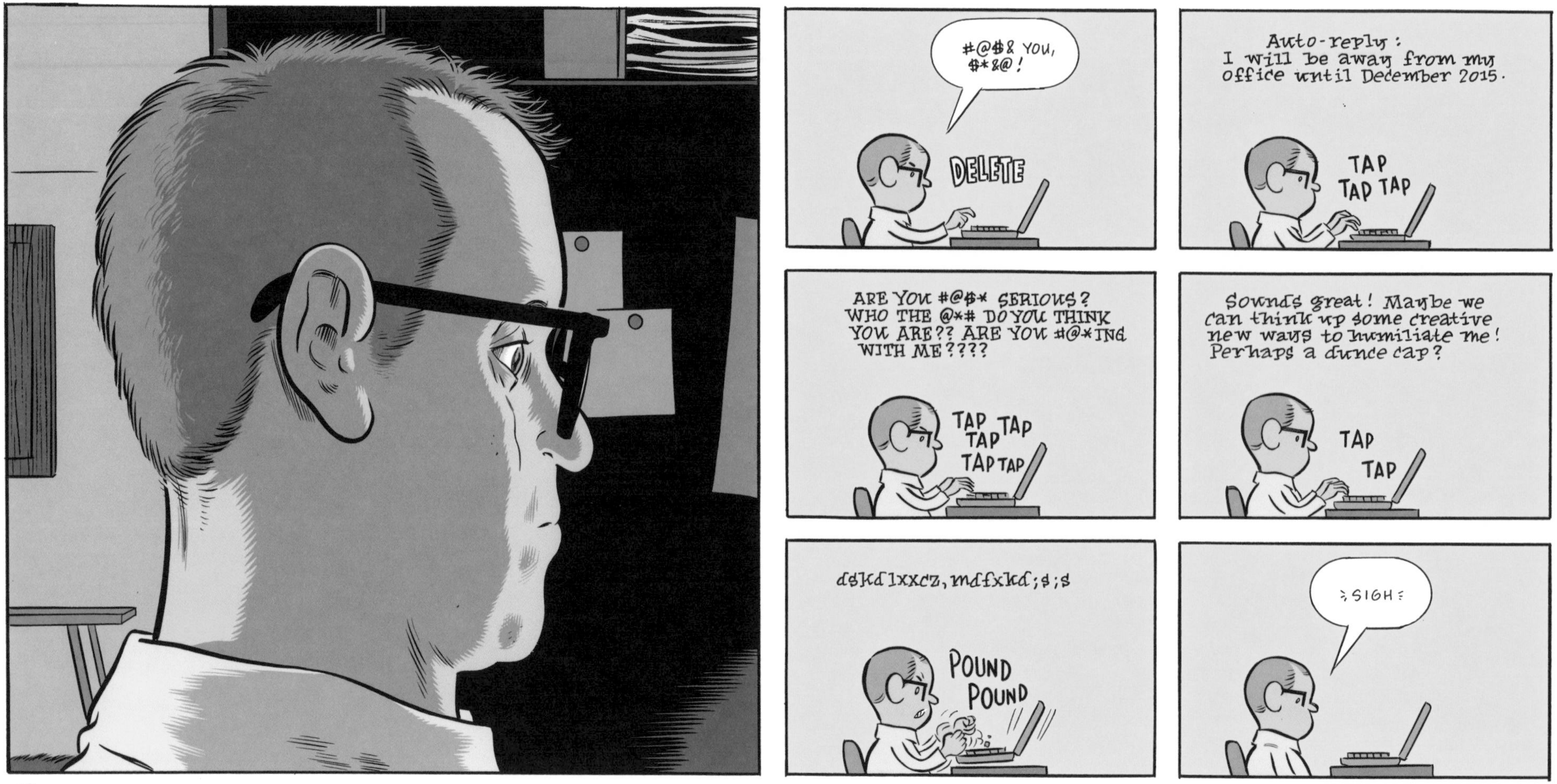
#@$& YOU, $*&@!
DELETE
Auto-reply: I will be away from my office until December 2015.
TAP TAP TAP
ARE YOU #@$* SERIOUS? WHO THE @*# DO YOU THINK YOU ARE?? ARE YOU #@*ING WITH ME????
TAP TAP TAP TAP TAP
Sounds great! Maybe we can think up some creative new ways to humiliate me! Perhaps a dunce cap?
TAP TAP
dskdlxxcz, mdfxkd;$;s
POUND POUND
SIGH

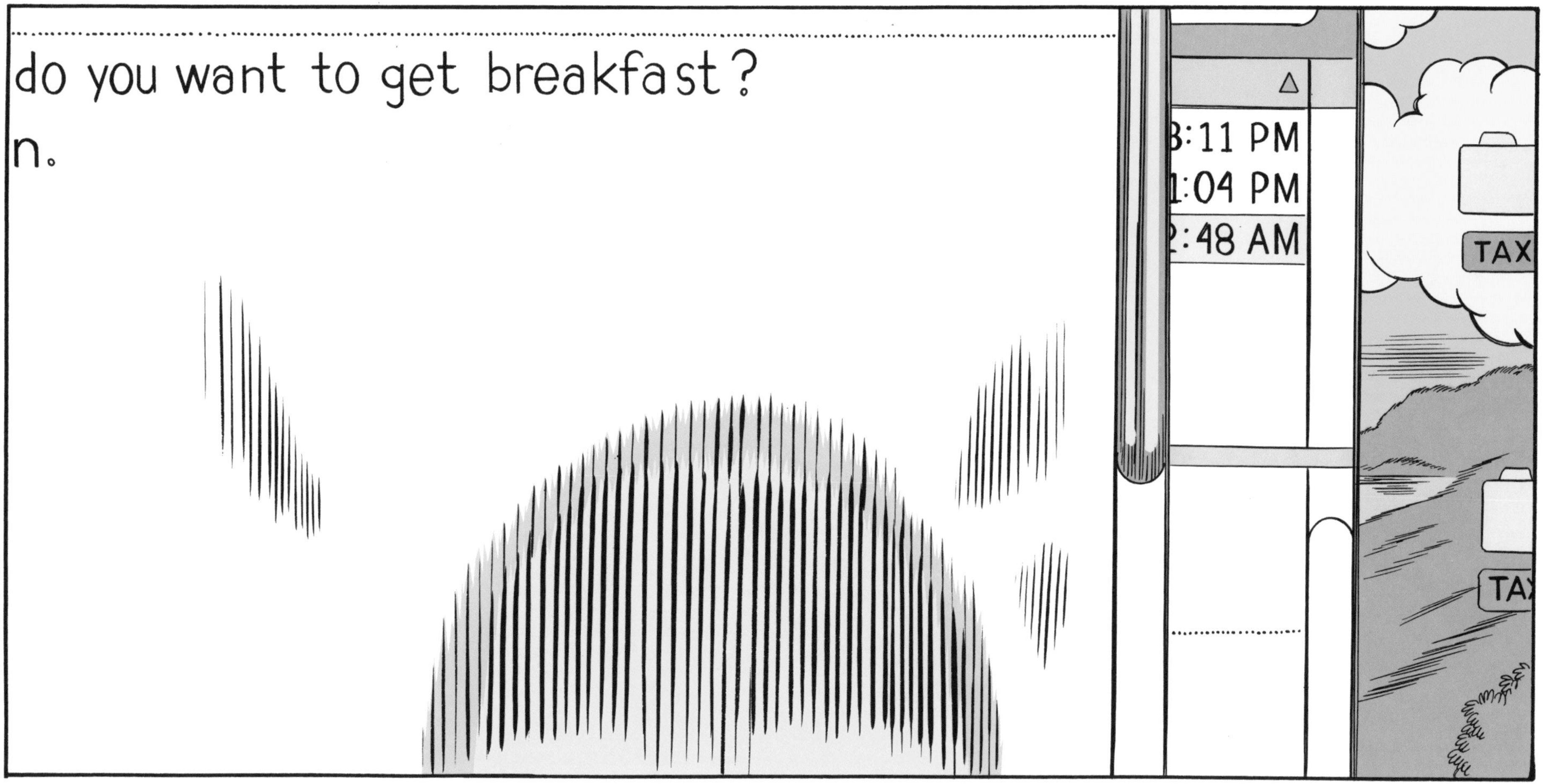
do you want to get breakfast?
n.
3:11 PM
1:04 PM
2:48 AM
TAX
TA

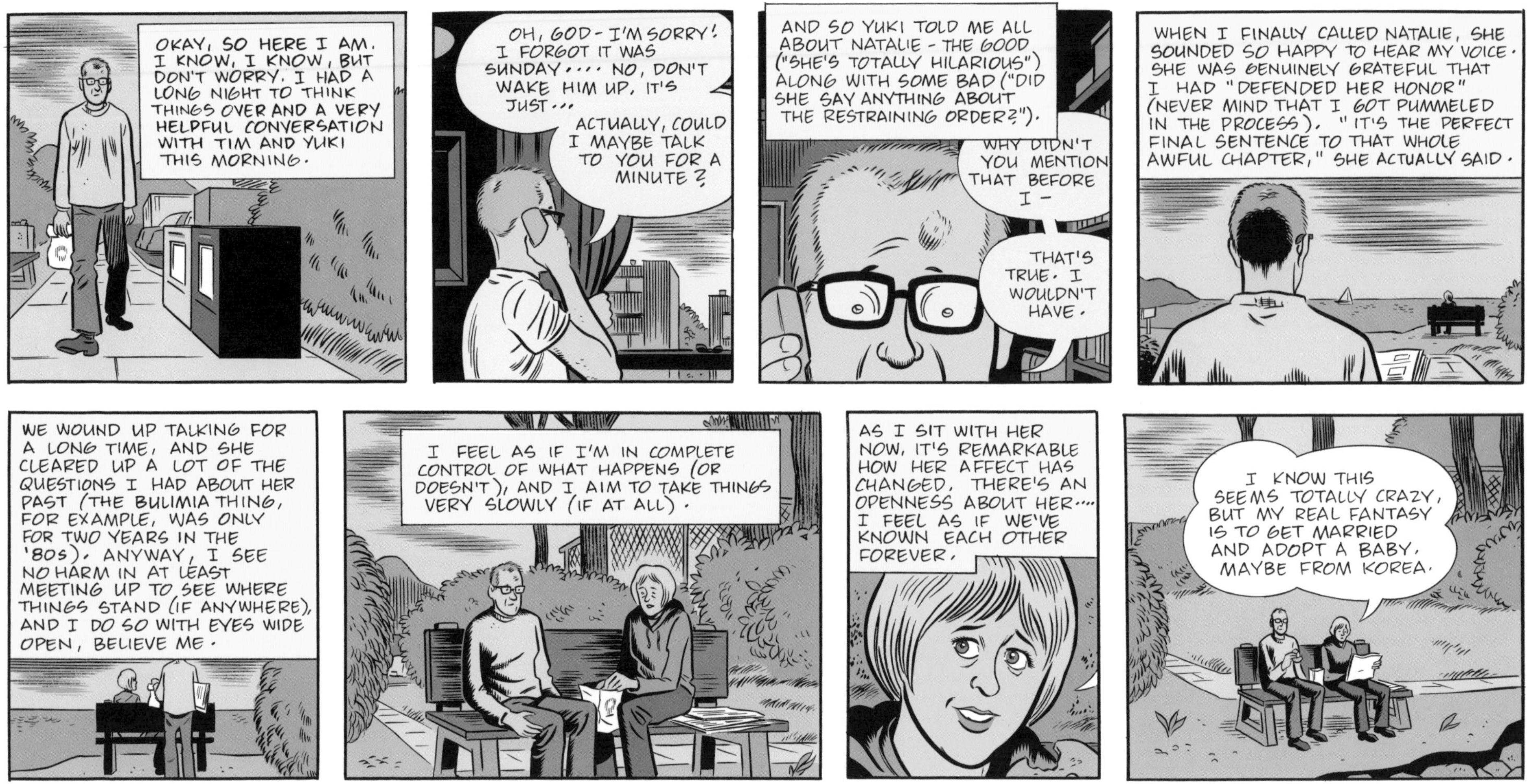
OKAY, SO HERE I AM. I KNOW, I KNOW, BUT DON'T WORRY. I HAD A LONG NIGHT TO THINK THINGS OVER AND A VERY HELPFUL CONVERSATION WITH TIM AND YUKI THIS MORNING.
OH, GOD - I'M SORRY! I FORGOT IT WAS SUNDAY.... NO, DON'T WAKE HIM UP, IT'S JUST...
ACTUALLY, COULD I MAYBE TALK TO YOU FOR A MINUTE?
AND SO YUKI TOLD ME ALL ABOUT NATALIE - THE GOOD ("SHE'S TOTALLY HILARIOUS") ALONG WITH SOME BAD ("DID SHE SAY ANYTHING ABOUT THE RESTRAINING ORDER?").
WHY DIDN'T YOU MENTION THAT BEFORE I -
THAT'S TRUE. I WOULDN'T HAVE.
WHEN I FINALLY CALLED NATALIE, SHE SOUNDED SO HAPPY TO HEAR MY VOICE. SHE WAS GENUINELY GRATEFUL THAT I HAD "DEFENDED HER HONOR" (NEVER MIND THAT I GOT PUMMELED IN THE PROCESS). "IT'S THE PERFECT FINAL SENTENCE TO THAT WHOLE AWFUL CHAPTER," SHE ACTUALLY SAID.
WE WOUND UP TALKING FOR A LONG TIME, AND SHE CLEARED UP A LOT OF THE QUESTIONS I HAD ABOUT HER PAST (THE BULIMIA THING, FOR EXAMPLE, WAS ONLY FOR TWO YEARS IN THE '80S). ANYWAY, I SEE NO HARM IN AT LEAST MEETING UP TO SEE WHERE THINGS STAND (IF ANYWHERE), AND I DO SO WITH EYES WIDE OPEN, BELIEVE ME.
I FEEL AS IF I'M IN COMPLETE CONTROL OF WHAT HAPPENS (OR DOESN'T), AND I AIM TO TAKE THINGS VERY SLOWLY (IF AT ALL).
AS I SIT WITH HER NOW, IT'S REMARKABLE HOW HER AFFECT HAS CHANGED. THERE'S AN OPENNESS ABOUT HER.... I FEEL AS IF WE'VE KNOWN EACH OTHER FOREVER.
I KNOW THIS SEEMS TOTALLY CRAZY, BUT MY REAL FANTASY IS TO GET MARRIED AND ADOPT A BABY. MAYBE FROM KOREA.

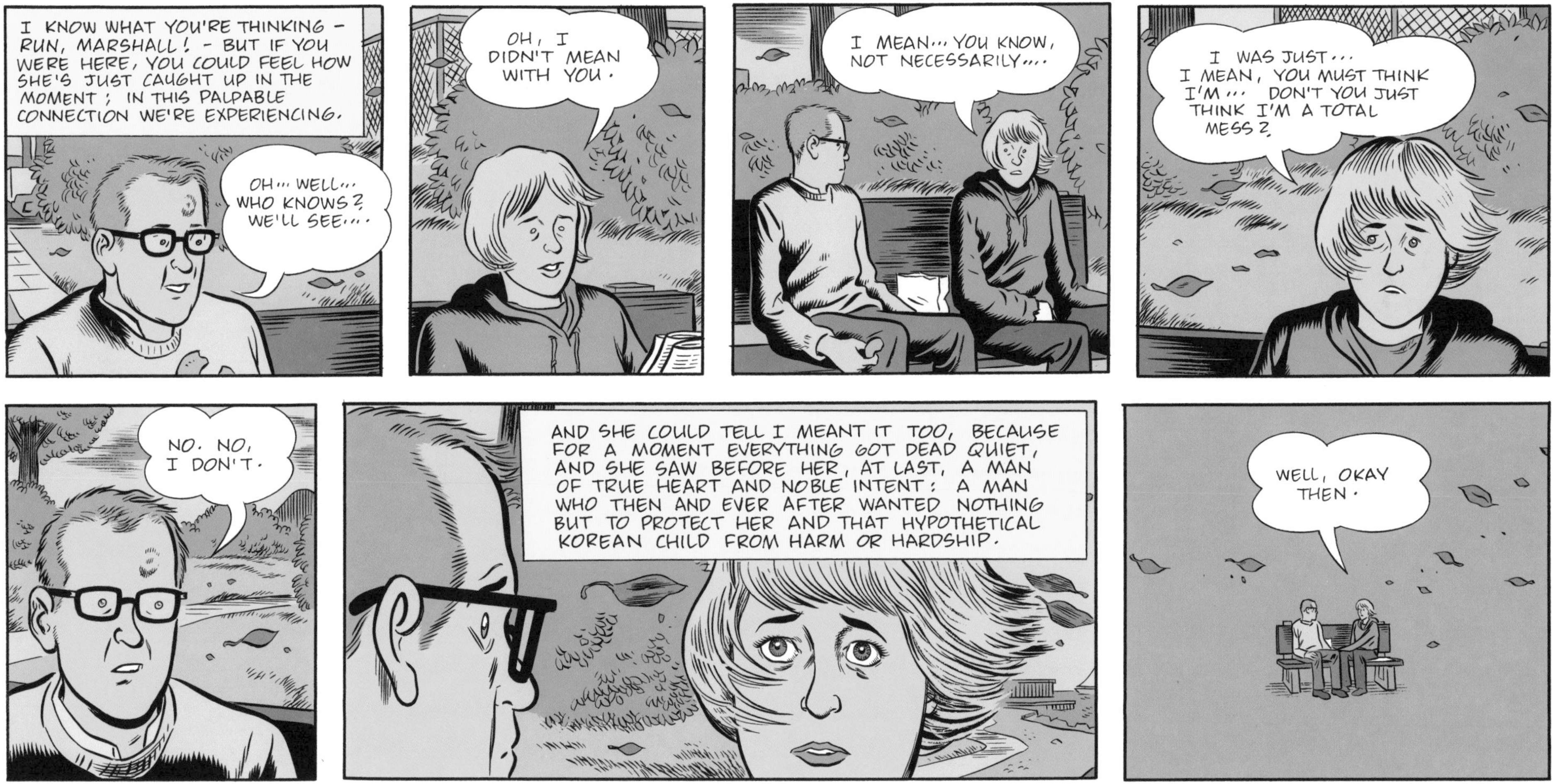
I KNOW WHAT YOU'RE THINKING - RUN, MARSHALL! - BUT IF YOU WERE HERE, YOU COULD FEEL HOW SHE'S JUST CAUGHT UP IN THE MOMENT; IN THIS PALPABLE CONNECTION WE'RE EXPERIENCING.
OH... WELL... WHO KNOWS? WE'LL SEE....
OH, I DIDN'T MEAN WITH YOU.
I MEAN... YOU KNOW, NOT NECESSARILY....
I WAS JUST... I MEAN, YOU MUST THINK I'M... DON'T YOU JUST THINK I'M A TOTAL MESS?
NO. NO, I DON'T.
AND SHE COULD TELL I MEANT IT TOO, BECAUSE FOR A MOMENT EVERYTHING GOT DEAD QUIET, AND SHE SAW BEFORE HER, AT LAST, A MAN OF TRUE HEART AND NOBLE INTENT: A MAN WHO THEN AND EVER AFTER WANTED NOTHING BUT TO PROTECT HER AND THAT HYPOTHETICAL KOREAN CHILD FROM HARM OR HARDSHIP.
WELL, OKAY THEN.

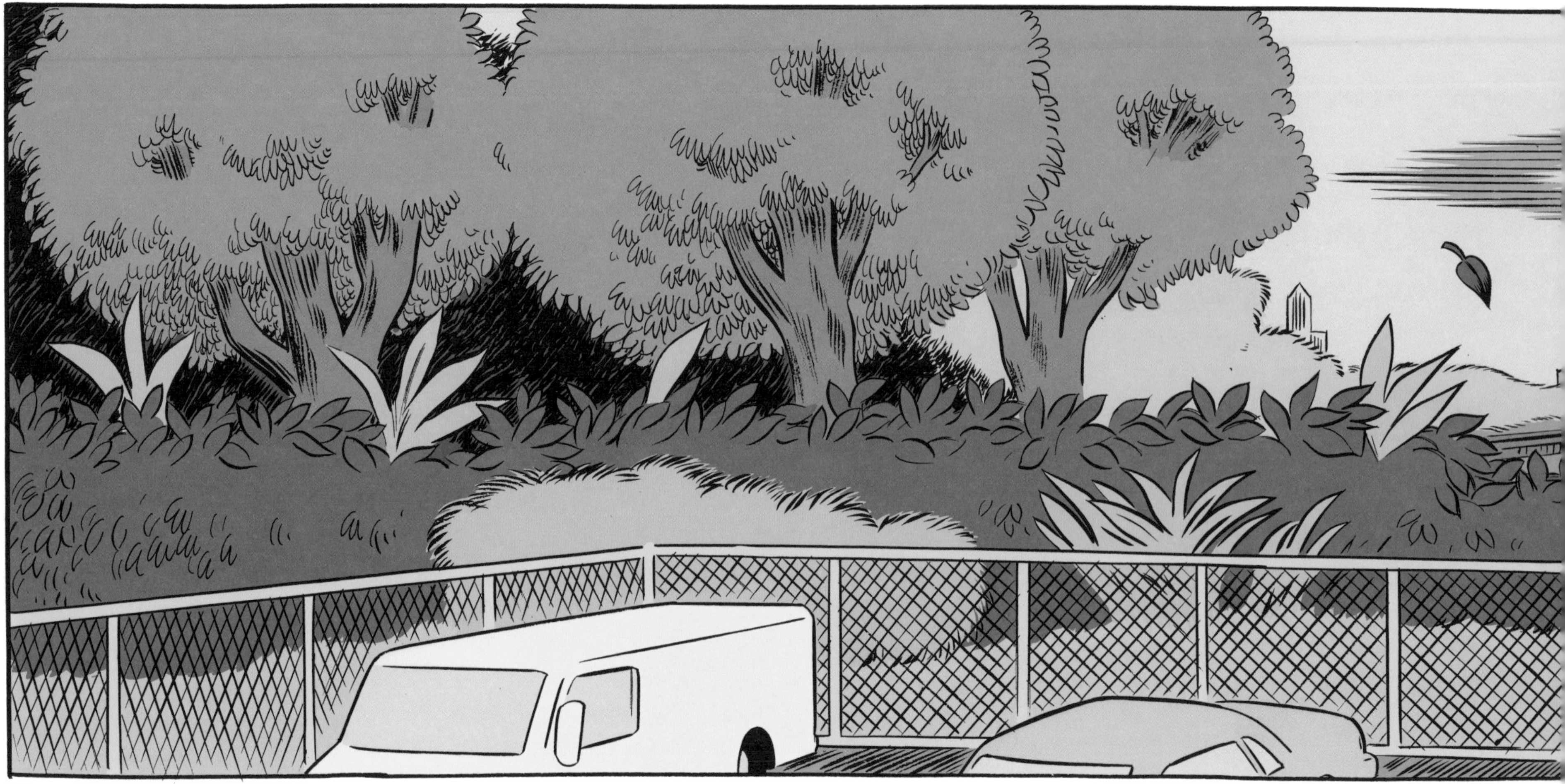

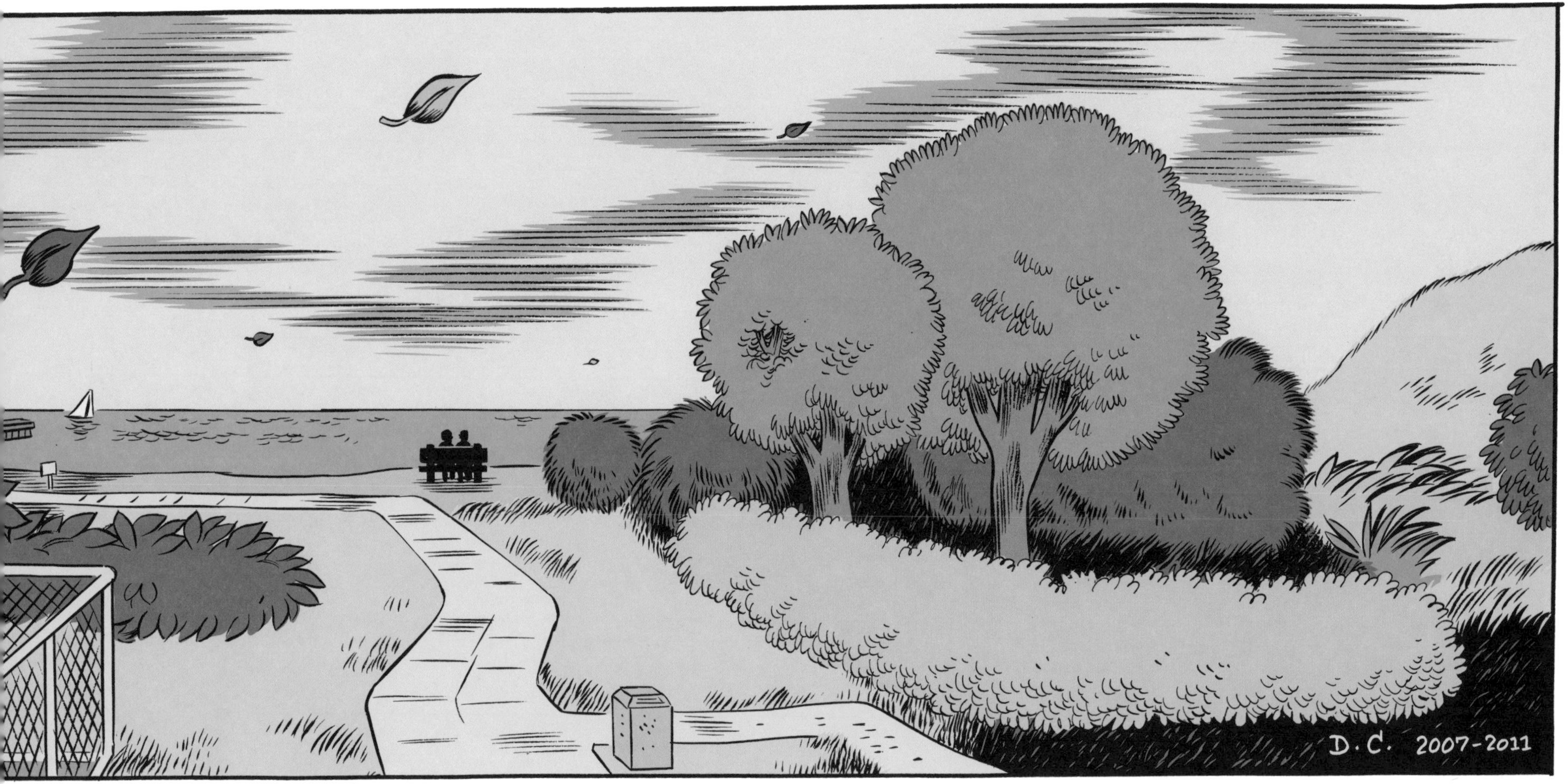
D.C. 2007-2011

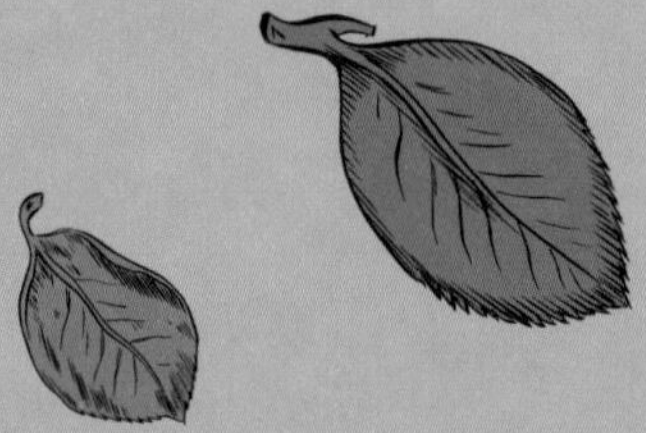